MINNESOTA'S OUTDOOR WONDERS

MINNESOTA'S OUTDOOR WONDERS

Exploring the Wonders of Minnesota

Month by Month

Jim Gilbert

with photos by David Brislance

NODIN PRESS

ISBN: 978-1-935666-42-4

Library of Congress Control Number: 2012945852

Front cover photos:
Marsh marigolds—Jim Gilbert
Lake Superior coast, red squirrel, autumn leaves, magnolia warbler—David Brislance
frontispiece: Jonvick Creek near Lutsen—David Brislance

Northern pike image, p. 63 © Pipa100 | Dreamstime.com

Book design and layout: John Toren

Printed at Bang Printing, Brainerd, Minnesota, USA

Nodin Press
530 North 3rd Street
Suite 120
Minneapolis, MN
55401

To my dear wife Sandra and our
four grandchildren—Lukas, Ailsa, Anja, and Lonne—
as they continue to discover the beauty of the world we live in.

This book is also dedicated to all who find pleasure in
small and large encounters with nature.

Acknowledgements

My thanks to publisher Norton Stillman who is aware of the wonders of nature and the joy of gardening. He has once again encouraged me to write some of my observations with hope that the book will help others to develop a sense of ecological understanding and stewardship. Norton is fortunate each year to celebrate his birthday on Earth Day, April 22.

John Toren is another person who lives his life close to nature, whether feeding wild birds in his wooded Minneapolis backyard or camping, biking, and canoeing with his wife Hilary in far-flung corners of the state. I'm pleased that he served as editor and designer for this volume and thank him for his skills.

David Brislance, from Lutsen, is a keen observer of the natural world, a trained artist, and an educator; all of which come out in his passion as a wildlife photographer. I thank him for his many fine images that have become the cornerstone for this publication.

What a privilege it has been for me to walk the trails and visit the various plant collections and natural areas of the University of Minnesota Landscape Arboretum, and to share observations with administrators, gardeners, naturalists, volunteers, and visitors for more than forty years. In putting this work together, I'm truly grateful for the use of the resources of the Andersen Horticultural Library at the Arboretum where staff members Katherine Allen, Christine Aho, Renee Jensen, and Susan Moe have provided key reference materials and a quiet study environment.

Without effective parents, a loving family, good teachers, and the chance to interact with countless people who find the natural world fascinating there is no way that I could have enjoyed a career as a naturalist. I'm truly blessed.

– Jim Gilbert, August 1, 2012

Contents

Introduction

The greatest show on earth is just outside our doors and windows. Life is full of wonders if we only open up our eyes and use our other senses.

A child's world is fresh and new and beautiful, full of wonder and excitement. It is my hope for children everywhere that they have the chance to develop a sense of wonder so indestructible that it will serve them well throughout their lives, freeing them from the curse of boredom and buoying their enthusiasm at times when an unfruitful preoccupation with artificial things may threaten to cut them off from the energy and beauty of the natural world. As the thirteenth-century Italian poet said, "Nature is the art of God."

For us adults, to hold onto and enhance the sense of wonder, we simply need to look up at the sky with its daily sunrise, moving clouds, vast blue, and stars at night. Listen to the falling rain and the calling crickets, enjoy feeling the wind, taste wild blueberries, and ponder the elegance of growing trees and the strength of hard-working ants in sidewalk cracks. Over the months watch the changing seasons, anticipate with delight the first spring American robin as well as the first autumn snowfall, and think about the miracle of migration as a flock of birds passes overhead.

This book, in words and images, attempts to capture the essence of the marvels we can observe, centered on Minnesota, both north and south. Hopefully it will remind us of nature's wonders throughout the earth and the importance of keeping the planet healthy, clean, and safe for future generations. We can never have world peace when we exploit the environment.

Daffodils at the University of Minnesota Landscape Arboretum.
photo by Jim Gilbert.

Minnesota's Outdoor Wonders

Pumpkin fields near Watertown. Photo by Jim Gilbert.

The planet Earth is in an elliptical orbit as it travels around the Sun each year. It happens that the Earth is closer to the Sun by 3.1 million miles on January 4 than on July 4. In spite of Minnesota being closest to the Sun in January, it nevertheless averages out as the coldest month of the year. Yet fleeting signs of spring are already in the air. During January in the Northern Hemisphere, the Sun is low in the sky. Days are warmer in the spring, summer, and fall in Minnesota because the Sun is higher in the sky, concentrating more heat on each acre of land or water. The days are also longer, giving the sun more time to heat the land and water, which then heats the atmosphere.

So, what's happening outdoors in January? The frozen land contributes ice and snow art. The dazzling sunlight on a morning after a snowstorm that covered and smoothed out the blemishes of our city and country landscapes gives us that unused look. Fresh snow is a blank page on which animals write their winter stories. Even in urban areas, the prints of squirrels, rabbits, house sparrows, dark-eyed juncos and other wild animals can be

JANUARY

numerous. Once you start looking, it's amazing the stories you can read.

Watching nuthatches, blue jays, and woodpeckers at a feeding station doesn't warm the day, but their actions warm the heart. Pine siskins or common redpolls could arrive on feeders at any time. The birdfeeder birds are around day after day, a reminder that life outlasts every winter. Think about the land-hibernating frogs—wood frogs, chorus frogs, spring peepers, and gray tree frogs—lying frozen yet still alive. See how evergreens—pines, spruces and firs—grace the winter scene with their shades of green. In Minnesota neighborhoods, after the maples and ashes have dropped their leaves, the evergreens give us bulk; they protect from the cold winds, provide privacy, and make us feel sheltered.

The days are short and nights long, but our daylight time increases almost an hour this month, and we often experience a warmer period or periods, known as "January thaws." With a thaw look for some mosses that will be lush green and growing, and honey bees out on cleansing flights, bicycle use on the upswing, and runners out in shorts.

Meteorologist Paul Douglas wrote in his January 21, 2012, *Minneapolis Star Tribune* column concerning the evidence of our incredible shrinking winters: "Winters in Minnesota have grown milder since 1998, with a steep reduction in Arctic air that was common 20 or 30 years ago. It's a slow-motion evolution." That's something for all of us to ponder.

If you are able, embrace this month of frozen elegance and go outside where you can feel the crunch of snow, gaze at tree silhouettes, and listen for quiet sounds such as the whistled "fee-bee" spring song of the black-capped chickadee telling us that one season slides slowly into the next.

photo: David Brislance

Coming from the Arctic where they nest, COMMON RED-POLLS are regular winter visitors in the northern and central regions of the state. We call it an invasion year when food is scarce in the far North and more of these winter finches come into Minnesota, and are even seen in the southern tier of counties. Then these irruptive 5-inch-long balls of feathers, with strongly forked tails and red caps, could appear at feeding stations most any place in the state. At feeders they like thistle seed and sunflower seed bits. On their own they feed on seeds from trees, shrubs, and plants in open fields.

Redpolls can survive colder temperatures better than most other songbirds. They store extra food in their crops and eat it at night to keep themselves warm. Seeds from ALDER cones are also important in the diet of redpolls. Speckled alder, along with paper birch, quaking aspen, and balsam poplar, can tolerate temperatures down to minus 80 degrees F. They do this by what is called extracellular freezing. By taking most of the liquid out of their cells and allowing it to freeze in spaces between the cells, the living tissue escapes being killed by the cold. Conifers such as tamarack, jack pine, balsam fir, white spruce, and black spruce can do the same thing.

Common goldeneye ducks wintering in the icy waters of Lake Superior at the harbor in Grand Marais.

Time to dig out the driveway after a big snowstorm.

photo: Jim Gilbert

photo: David Brislance

photo: Jim Gilbert

photo: David Brislance

Surrounded by neighbors on Lake Waconia, or enjoying the wildness of Trout Lake off the Gunflint Trail in Cook County—in either case, many Minnesotans relish dropping a line, regardless of the temperature.

photo: Jim Gilbert

Trees cast long shadows in the low January sun.

The splendid WHITE FROST (right) also called hoar frost, is created when nights are clear and calm, and air next to the surface is relatively moist. If the surface temperatures of objects stay above freezing under these conditions, dew is likely to form. As water in a gas form changes to a solid form, interlocking ice crystals eventually build up on objects exposed to the frigid night air, transforming a landscape of trees, shrubs, fences, and utility wires into an awesome winter scene. The clear blue morning sky and white frost-covered countryside or cityscape brings out photographers and others who appreciate nature's beauty.

photo: Jim Gilbert

A team of "canine athletes" and their musher in a John Beargrease race along the North Shore.

A Bohemian waxwing eats fruit from a native mountain ash at Grand Marais. The fruit is usually abundant and stays on the trees all winter, serving as a critical food source for migrating and resident bird species.

Bohemian waxwings are winter visitors in Minnesota, most often encountered in the northern parts of the state where there is an abundance of mountain ash or ornamental crabapple trees. Their flocks move about as food supplies are exhausted.

photos: David Brislance

The John Beargrease Sled Dog Marathon is an annual end-of-January competition covering a 390-mile route between Duluth and Poplar Lake near the Gunflint Trail and back. The race honors the accomplishments of John Beargrease, an Anishinabe man who delivered the weekly mail between Two Harbors and Grand Marais for almost 20 years until 1899, using a dog team in winter.

For a real winter adventure, try dog sledding through part of northern Minnesota's back country. Some of the best dog mushers in North America offer opportunities for interested beginners who would like to experience the sport.

photos: David Brislance

SOUNDS OF JANUARY

Already, during the first two weeks in January, three woodpecker species—downy, hairy and pileated—are heard drumming in response to lengthening days. They hammer on "signal posts," usually resonant tree trunks and branches, to announce territories and attract mates. Also at this time we listen for the "whi, whi, whi, ..." spring song of the white-breasted nuthatch, and blue jays are heard in their first noisy groups and vocalizing their special "pump-handle" spring call, also known as the "speelunker" call. All are great sounds!

Meanwhile, great homed owls continue duet hooting as they set up nesting territories, and by the end of the month the first eggs, typically two in a clutch, have been laid, usually in an old nest of a larger bird such as a red-tailed hawk, great blue heron, or American crow, and sometimes on top of a squirrel's nest. The great horned owl is the earliest nesting bird in Minnesota.

In 2011, I first heard the whistled "fee-bee" song of the BLACK-CAPPED CHICKADEE on January 6 at 8:30 a.m. The air temperature was +6 ° F, and it was sunny with very little wind here on the shore of Lake Waconia.

In a clear, sweet whistle, the chickadee sounds two notes of equal length, the second tone lower in pitch than the first, making a "fee-bee" sound. Frequently the second note has a slight waver in the middle, as if the bird sang a "fee-beyee" rather than "fee-bee."

Even on cold January mornings in northern Minnesota, we sometimes hear chickadees whistling "fee-bee" over and over. This sound lifts our spirits because it's considered one of the earliest spring signs. Some people even interpret the call as "spring-soon." It's a matter of speculation whether the "fee-bee" call is the true song of the chickadee. Yes, it's heard most often in early spring, but we can hear it throughout the winter, in the summer, and on crisp autumn days.

Some listeners confuse this song with the well-enunciated but rather coarse "phoe-be" or "fi-bree" of the eastern phoebe, which is croaked rather than whistled. The eastern phoebe is a summer resident, usually arriving in late March and leaving in September; you won't hear its call in January.

(above) A downy woodpecker.
(right) A pileated woodpecker.

GRAY WOLVES (left) also called timber wolves, once roamed across most of North America. Now they're found only in sparsely settled parts of Alaska, Canada, Montana, northern Minnesota, Wisconsin, and Michigan. They can vary in color from white to black, but most often are predominantly gray. Gray wolves are the largest wild dog species, with adults ranging in weight from 55 to 130 pounds.

Wolves are social, living in packs of a few to a dozen —mostly family members. They mark their territories with urine and feces, and howl to announce their whereabouts.

The pack ranges over a territory that covers about 100 to 300 square miles, making the gray wolf one of the most mobile animals. An estimated 3,000 wolves were living in Minnesota as of January 2012. It's a thrill and a privilege to see one in the wild. Gray wolves mate near the end of February, and sixty-three days later they produce from one to seven young. Usually only a single pair in the pack breeds.

Being omnivores, wolves eat small to large animals such as insects, mice, hares, fish, deer, and moose, but also wild fruits and other plant material. There are no confirmed instances of wolves killing or injuring people in Minnesota.

photos: David Brislance

A resident of northern Minnesota's evergreen forests, SNOWSHOE HARES (above) are dark brown during the summer. They turn white in winter but keep their black-tipped ears. These hares are known for their long ears and large hind feet—the "snowshoes" that enable them to move across the snow-covered landscape. Food consists of green plants and fruit in summer, and in winter the bark and buds of deciduous woody plants plus evergreen needles.

Deep snow is an advantage for hares; they can move fast on top of it, and heavy snows bend down branches, making life for these small browsers much easier. Winter must certainly be the snowshoe's favorite season.

Snowshoe hares are members of the rabbit and hare family. Young hares are born having a fur coat and open eyes, and they are able to run within hours of birth. Rabbits, like the eastern cottontail of southern Minnesota, are born naked and with their eyes shut, and do not turn white in the winter.

A wolf track in the snow.

A forest dweller, the FISHER is found mostly in the northern part of the state. It's the largest member of the weasel family and about the size of a fox. Active day and night, these largely solitary animals hunt during sporadic bursts of activity that last a few hours. They feed on snowshoe hares, red squirrels, mice, and birds; but also on berries, nuts, and other plant matter. They are one of the few predators with the wherewithal to bring down porcupines consistently.

A fisher doesn't have a regular den. It's constantly on the move across a territory ranging up to 30 square miles, but it may seek a tree cavity or other shelter to rest for a couple of days during bad winter weather.

A fisher's fur changes color somewhat with the seasons, but it's usually a deep brown. The female's fur is silkier. Despite the name, the fisher does not fish. Maybe the name came from people mistaking it for its smaller cousin, the mink, which is a good fisher.

photo: David Brislance

photo: Jim Gilbert

In mid-winter 2012, a birder from the Rice area, north of St. Cloud, called to tell me he had just counted fifty-seven WILD TURKEYS in his yard. I have seen a flock of about a hundred near St. Peter. Standing three to four feet tall and weighing from 8 to 18 pounds, wild turkeys are likely to be the largest birds attracted to backyard feeding stations. They like cracked and whole corn. These large birds roost high up in trees at night.

There is no positive evidence that this species lived in Minnesota before European settlement, but they were introduced into the southern part of the state as far back as 1936. Now, after a series of re-introduction efforts in the 1960s and 70s, they're permanent residents in some woodlands and along forest edges, mostly across the southern third of the state. As winters grow milder, they continue to expand their range. Minnesota's wild turkey population grew from a few small flocks in the 1970s to about 60,000 birds by 2006.

The bird from which the domestic turkey was bred almost became our national bird, losing out to the bald eagle by a single vote in 1782.

A male northern cardinal in a snowstorm

photo: Jim Gilbert

A common bird of the southern and eastern United States, the NORTHERN CARDINAL (above) is expanding its range northward. They're permanent residents in most of southern Minnesota, and a few make their homes in the north. They prefer woodland edges, open woods, parks, and backyards with plenty of trees and shrubs for cover. Cardinals often visit feeding stations; sunflower seeds are a favorite but they also relish cracked corn scattered on the ground.

Cardinal's are known to mate for life. During late spring and all summer we see them in pairs as they defend their breeding territories of about three acres, but each pair is also part of a larger community , and when their territories break down in winter weather a dozen or more birds may flock together, all coming to a feeding station at once.

Each year a very few northern cardinals are heard singing the rich, whistled "what-cheer, cheer, cheer" songs in January. (In 2012 I first heard it on January 4.) By mid-February these 9-inch long songsters are singing loud and long. There are many variations of the song, such as "what-cheer, cheer, cheer, birdie-birdie, birdie," and "cheer, cheer, wit, wit, wit, wit, wit, wit, wit." Both sexes sing these territorial songs—sometimes together.

So, the very early start of the nesting season is marked by renewed singing. As a courtship gesture, the male often feeds the female. In late winter we'll notice this mate-feeding at feeding stations. This is also the time when a cardinal may start to respond to its reflection in a window, displaying and attempting to drive away a bird it thinks is an intruder. Both sexes do this. Mobiles or sunlight-reflecting ribbon tape hung from an eave can help break up these futile gestures.

When northern cardinals get infected with feather mites on the head—an area they can't reach to preen—they may lose these feathers and look bald. Once the mites leave, the head feathers grow back in and the bird looks normal again.

The hawk owl is an uncommon winter visitor to the northeastern region of the state.

February is often the most pleasant month of winter, mainly due to the 80 minutes of added daylight we receive as the month proceeds. Lakes are normally covered by at least 18 to 24 inches of ice—but always respect changing conditions and be careful. After a snowfall, tracking should be good. It's fun to get out and see who goes where, to note the activities of neighborhood gray squirrels, cottontail rabbits, and tunneling shrews, all recorded in the snow. In southern Minnesota, wintering mourning doves are fairly common at feeding stations where they prefer to eat cracked corn and other seeds scattered on the ground. Up north, pine siskins and pine grosbeaks visit sunflower feeders. Just before and during snowfalls, you can watch the birds at feeders in their "feeding frenzy" mode.

Between now and the end of March is a good time to prune grape vines and to continue pruning apple trees and oaks. It's time for colorful displays of garden vegetable and flower seed

FEBRUARY

packets to appear in grocery stores. Begonia and geranium seeds should be started indoors by the second week of February.

Raccoons and skunks come out during warm spells, searching for food and companionship. By mid-month the mating season has started for flying, fox, gray, and red squirrels. Red foxes are normally solitary but can now be observed in pairs as their mating season approaches. Minnesota is unique among the contiguous 48 states because of its large timber wolf population of about 3,000. They are the living symbol of the wilderness, and this is their month to mate. Watch for horned larks, one of our first returning migrants, along country roads in southern and western Minnesota; in the north newborn black bear cubs nestle close to their slumbering mothers and common ravens start nest building.

Those of us who are close to nature during the length of a Minnesota winter can sincerely appreciate even the subtle spring signs and take joy in each happening. The wonderful whistled songs of the northern cardinal make us take note. Our minds think of warmer days. American goldfinches show more yellow coloration as the nesting season approaches. Near the end of the month listen for mourning doves to begin cooing, and male courting ring-necked pheasants to start crowing their loud double squawks.

photo: David Brislance

Blue Jays are permanent residents throughout Minnesota, but many of these birds, especially those nesting in the north, head southward out of the state in early fall, traveling by daylight in flocks of ten or more. Being about a foot long, mostly blue and crested, they are unmistakable. Male and female blue jays look alike. They are smart, adaptable and vocal. Besides the noisy 'jaay, jaay" call, they made a variety of squeaks, rattles, and croaks, even screaming like a hawk, which causes other birds to scatter as they approach a bird feeder. While a single blue jay may bury thousands of acorns over the years, many are never retrieved, so jays are credited with helping to regenerate forests. Being omnivores, blue jays eat berries, acorns and other seeds, insects, spiders, snails, frogs, small fish, and bird eggs and chicks, plus a variety of human-supplied foods. Sometimes persecuted by humans as nest robbers or bullies at feeding stations, they also should be credited with alerting other birds and small mammals to the presence of hawks, owls, and other enemies.

A blue jay's feathers don't have blue pigment, but look blue due to the refraction (bending of light waves) of sunlight off their irregular surfaces.

Full Moon over Lake Superior at Split Rock Lighthouse, February 7, 2012.

photos: David Brislance

An American crow on the shores of frigid Lake Superior hesitates, then finally takes a plunge.

photo: Christian Gilbert

THE GLORIOUS NORTH SHORE

Lutsen Mountains (left), rising more than 1,000 feet over the surface of Lake Superior, offers sweeping runs for skiers and boarders, with the breathtaking beauty of the North Shore below. The area can get more than nine feet of snow in a winter, ensuring a ski season that lasts into the first week of April.

PINE SISKINS are considered to be winter finches in central and southern Minnesota, but they're scarce in some years. They're year-round residents in the northeastern third of the state.

Males and females look alike. These five-inch, brown, streaked birds have yellow wing stripes and tail spots, though they aren't always apparent. The slender, pointy beak is also characteristic. Siskins eat seeds, berries, and insects, and will come to seed feeders sometimes by the dozens. They relish sunflower bits and thistle seed, and are frequently spotted amid flocks of common redpolls and the drab winter American goldfinches. Listen for the sharp, zippy calls of pine siskin flocks as they fly overhead.

Male pine siskins begin courting females in late winter. They're known to nest in loose colonies in conifer or mixed conifer-deciduous forests, often only a few feet apart.

photos: David Brislance

(above) Pine siskins in a feeding frenzy during a snowstorm at Lutsen.

(left) Note the faint yellow streak on the edge of the pine siskin's wing.

The SNOWY OWL is a fairly regular winter migrant and visitor in northern Minnesota. They are almost always encountered as individuals. They come south into Minnesota from the arctic tundra of Canada when food is in short supply. About every four years an invasion of these birds sends a few individuals as far south as the Iowa border.

The Duluth/Superior area is the most reliable place to see snowy owls, especially around grain elevators and railroad tracks where spilled grain feeds mice, rats, and pigeons, which in turn can become food for snowies.

A female snowy owl has heavy brown-gray bars across her wings and body; males are pure white with a few dark spots on their bodies and wings.

A snowy owl at the Duluth/Superior Harbor.

photos: David Brislance

An active birdfeeder just off the Caribou Trail near Lutsen. Pine grosbeaks and others relish the seeds.

BIRDS OF FEBRUARY

The **COMMON RAVEN, a** bird the size of a hawk, is common only in wilderness areas. It is very sensitive to human persecution and has long since been driven out of settled areas by shooting and poisoning. Raven pairs can often be seen soaring like eagles. They also perform wonderful aerial acrobatics and long swooping dives. They produce rasping "kronk-kronk" calls quite different from the high-pitched caws of American crows. However, both these species have multi-varied vocalizations. The raven is larger than the crow. Both are all black, but the crow lacks the raven's large head and bill, and shaggy throat feathers. A year-round resident in Minnesota, where it lives mostly in the northeast quarter of the state, the common raven is one of the earliest birds to nest each year. Nest building or repair begins in February.

Ravens are known to use the same nest site for many years and to mate for life. They're scavengers, eating insects, fruit, small animals, and carrion (dead meat). Frequently they hang around wolf packs where they provide the wolves with extra protection using their keen eyesight, and the wolves in turn provide the ravens with leftover food.

The **PINE GROSBEAK** (right) is a nine-inch-long finch that can be seen in northeastern and north central Minnesota in most years. Their loud, whistled notes can brighten even the coldest February day. They are birds of the spruce-fir forest, and feed on seeds, buds, fruit and insects; and will come to feeders. Pine grosbeaks have long tails, stubby black bills and two wing bars. Adult males look rosy-red and gray overall, while females are tinged with dull yellow on their heads and rumps.

photos: David Brislance

photo: Jim Gilbert

Snow on a Colorado blue spruce.

Snow on a COLORADO BLUE SPRUCE (left). When we look at the winter landscape, it's the snow that contributes most to its beauty. Snow on evergreen boughs is one of the most splendid sights of nature. We can expect to see snow on spruces, firs, and pines for about thirty days each year. Winds and thaws remove the snow during the rest of winter.

BALD EAGLES (right) are diurnal, active during the day and resting at night. A good share of them depart in the fall for the southern states. Those that winter over can be found around areas of open water such as the Mississippi River and along the North Shore of Lake Superior.

This bird has made a comeback in Minnesota, which now has one of the largest breeding populations in the lower 48 states. As of early 2011, Minnesota was home to about 1,300 breeding pairs of bald eagles. Their nesting season begins in February. It is thought that they mate for life and return to the same nest each year, adding more sticks. A large nest could weigh 1,000 pounds and is usually in a tall tree. That's a big nest for only two 2½-inch-long eggs. Both female and male incubate the eggs that hatch in about 35 days. The young stay in the nest for about three months, and don't have full adult plumage, with white head and tail, until they reach four or five years of age.

While searching for food and migrating, bald eagles use their seven-foot wingspan to climb in flight and to glide and soar. These huge raptors are carnivorous, eating mostly fish, plus some birds and a few mammals and reptiles. Females and males look alike, but females are commonly slightly larger. The yellow eyes, large, curved, yellow bill, and yellow feet are distinctive.

In a midair mating ritual, one eagle will fly upside down and lock talons with another. Both will tumble, and then they break apart to continue their flights. [photo: David Brislance]

The bald eagle, the national symbol
of the United States.

photo: David Brislance

The coat is longer in winter, giving the deer a larger appearance, and the individual hairs, which are thick and hollow, provide effective winter insulation. The tail is distinctive for both sexes and all ages. It's brown above with white fringe and is entirely white

The **WHITE-TAILED DEER** is the most common large mammal in Minnesota. They can be found in many habitats throughout the state. Being active at night as well as during the daytime, deer don't use a den even in bad weather, but may choose a different spot to rest whenever they get tired. During a winter with snow it's easy to find their beds, which are often concentrated in maple/basswood forests. The deer in northern Minnesota also seek shelter under protective evergreens in black spruce and cedar swamps.

Deer are reddish-brown for three or four months in summer and grayish-brown in fall, winter and early spring.

below. A fleeting white-tailed deer identifies itself with its conspicuous upright white "flag."

White-tails eat leaves and twigs from shrubs and trees in summer; and in winter feed on twigs with buds, and on evergreen foliage. In season they also relish non-woody plants like grasses and wildflowers, mushrooms and fallen acorns, and glean corn kernels in harvested fields. Twigs browsed by deer are often ripped or torn because the animal lacks upper front teeth.

Deer are color blind, seeing the world in black and white. They are excellent swimmers, can jump up to 8½ feet high, leap 30 feet laterally, and run almost 40 miles per hour.

EARLY SIGNS OF SPRING

photo: Jim Gilbert

photo: David Brislance

A European starling (above).

Falling red oak leaves (below). The native red oak trees hold a good percentage of their leaves from last growing season, and when they drop in February it's considered a subtle spring sign.

photo: Jim Gilbert

On or close to February 11 each year, as the sun rises higher in the sky, plants in greenhouses come out of dormancy and start growing. In the Meyer-Deats Conservatory (above) at the University of Minnesota Landscape Arboretum, the bird of paradise and various orchids love the February sunlight. On sunny days after that date, greenhouses become hot and humid, and even on cold days, the interiors of our cars now warm up when parked in the sunlight.

The bill of the European starling (above right) changes from black to yellow in February for the nesting season. The starling in the photograph is eating fruit from a native mountain ash tree in Grand Marais. The starling itself is not native to the United States but was introduced to New York City from Europe in 1890.

The shelves of IGNEOUS ROCK on Lake Superior's North Shore were formed a billion years ago as lava poured out of a rift in the earth's surface. Since that time, wind, rain, and ice have slowly been wearing the rock away. Mosses, lichens, and other plants eventually gain footholds in the fissures that have been opened by the expanding and contracting ice.

BEAVERS spend the winter months under the ice, keeping warm in their dome-shaped houses and feeding on vegetation they cached underwater before the ponds froze. But they occasionally venture up into the sunlight during warm spells. Whoever started in on this freshly-gnawed tree in Foothills State Forest west of Bachus gave up on it; perhaps he'll be back in the spring to finish the job.

photos: John Toren

Minnesota is home to two noble species of pine, the red pine and the WHITE PINE (right). The red pine is Minnesota's state tree, but it was the white pine that brought lumbermen to the region from Michigan and Maine in the late nineteenth century. These truly spectacular pines are symbols of the North Woods, much like the loon. Most of the central and northern part of the state, which is now covered with aspen, sugar maple, paper birch, and jack pine, was at one time dotted with stands of such pines—many of them more than two-hundred feet tall.

Though the forest industy has long since leveled the gigantic first-growth pines, impressive remnants and second-growth forests still beautify the northern landscape. You can see them at Voyaguers National Park, Scenic State Park, and especially in the Boundary Waters Canoe Area Wilderness and Itasca State Park, which contains 25 percent of the state's remaining old-growth red and white pine forests, as well as Minnesota's record white pine and red pine. Many of the remaining old-growth stands were preserved by accident—the surveyors and timber cruisers who worked for the lumber barons missed them— though Itasca's giants were deliberately saved by concerned citizens. In Minnesota, only 15,000 acres remain of the original old-growth pine forest. That's less than 1 percent of the formerly vast forest that took hundreds of years to grow.

Pines can survive the cold winter months because their needle-shaped leaves minimize surface area and their waxy leaf coatings cut down on evaporation and help shed snow.

photo: John Toren

MARCH

Interesting changes occur in March. Stone and brick walls facing south actually feel warm on sunny days. We smell thawed mud, and on rainy days decaying leaves. Those with the good fortune to be in a sugarbush are able to taste cool, slightly sweet sap and fresh warm syrup. Even with new snowfalls we see quick-melting, fast-moving streams and temporary ponds. And the singing of birds increases manyfold in March, not only due to migrants returning north but also because the year 'round residents are responding to the increase in daylight.

For centuries people have believed that birds sing to announce the arrival of spring. But there is much more to the ritual of singing than that. It's important for birds to mark off territories and attract mates. Competition for nesting sites and food can be fierce, and birds often sing and also display themselves prominently, warning other birds of their own species that the territory has been taken. If too many American robins were in the same territory, earthworms and fruit would soon disappear. Birds don't need to be concerned about other species nesting in their territories if those other birds eat different foods. It's not unusual for a mallard, a black-capped chickadee, and an American robin to nest in the same vicinity, because they don't compete with one another for food.

March is a transition time when cold meets warm. It could be a snowy time, but by the end of the month, storms are more likely to bring rain than snow. We in southern Minnesota welcome back the first migrating red-winged blackbirds and wood ducks, while in the north deep snow usually covers the landscape, offering some of the best snowshoeing of the year.

An early male **American robin**. A small percentage of robins winter in Minnesota, even as far north as the shore of Lake Superior. In autumn most American robins migrate to the southern states and into Mexico. The first migrants to arrive back are males, and they are very flighty and noisy when they return in early- to mid-March into southern Minnesota; the timing depends on weather conditions. The first females usually appear about three weeks later.

It's easy to differentiate male and female American robins. The male has a dark, nearly black head and a bright red-brown breast; the female has a gray head and a pale red-brown breast.

photo: David Brislance

A mourning cloak butterfly.

photo: Jim Gilbert

(above) The long, arching, bright golden-yellow twigs make weeping willows glow on the landscape at Victoria.

(below) "Pancake Ice" in the harbor at Grand Marais. The ice chunks become rounded as they bump together in wave swells.

Minnesota is home to 172 species of butterflies, only nine of which overwinter in the adult stage. They hibernate under lose bark, in hollow logs and trees, under eaves or in unheated buildings, and may awaken and appear on the wing on a few March days when the temperature reaches 50°F. One of the nine, the attractive **MOURNING CLOAK BUTTERFLY,** has glossy chocolate-colored wings that are three inches wide and rimmed with blue spots and a yellowish-gold border. Adults of the mourning cloak that have hibernated may be seen during a warm spell in very early spring, sunning with open wings, and flying about searching for food—the sweet sap that drips from broken twigs of maple and birch trees. These overwintered mourning cloaks eventually produce a new generation, the adults of which appear in late June.

photo: Jim Gilbert

PHENOLOGY

Phenology is the recording of nature's calendar. Events such as arrival times of various migrating birds, lake ice-outs, apple trees blooming, harvest times for garden and farm crops, and tree leaves changing color in the fall are all examples of phenological events. The act of observing and recording these events draws individuals into a deeper relationship with their environment. Long-term phenology monitoring helps us keep track of the changing world. As an educator, I'm interested in getting people outdoors to become familiar with a few of the plants and animals, plus some physical features, of the natural world. I found personally, many years ago, that phenology was one of the best tools for me to become a good observer.

Spring, the awakening season, is a great time for someone young—or not so young—to begin a phenology journal or list of happenings. What follows is a suggested list that could become a starting point. Just record dates, add to the list and keep it going year after year, perhaps in a special notebook. Over time you'll develop a good perspective on what's happening in your own locality with regards to nature and climate.

ORGANISM OR PHYSICAL FEATURE	EVENT	DATE
1. Northern cardinal	First heard singing	
2. Red-winged blackbird	First sighting	
3. Ice-out (Name of lake)	Lake becomes 90% ice-free	
4. Common dandelion	First flower opens	
5. Thunderstorm	First lightning and thunder	
6. Bloodroot	First flower	
7. Common purple lilac	Peak of bloom	
8. Canada goose	First goslings seen	
9. Sugar maple	First leaves emerging	
10. Ruby-throated hummingbird	First sighting	

photos: Jim Gilbert

(above) Tapped sugar maple trees, showing blue bag to collect sap and tube network to collect sap from several trees.

(right) Catching a drop of maple sap.

Maple sap flow is triggered by thawing days following freezing nights. In southern Minnesota the best flows tend to come between March and the first few days of April, at which point leaf buds swell and sap becomes bitter. The best flows often occur when a frosty night is followed by a sunny day with temperatures reaching into the 40s or higher. Late afternoon is a good time to collect the day's flow.

The sap will flow from any wound in the sapwood—a hole bored into the tree or a broken twig. Sugar maples, black maples, and box elders, also known as ash-leaved maples, are best for tapping. The red maple and silver maple can also be tapped but their sap is less sweet. A forest of many maple trees together is called a sugarbush. Maples are tapped using a carpenter's brace with a ⅜ inch bit. Trunks smaller than 10 inches should not be tapped. Holes two inches deep are bored into the tree trunk about three feet above ground. A small metal or wooden tube called a spile is inserted into

the hole and tapped slightly with a hammer so it fits snugly. The spile supports the container and carries sap into it.

Maple syrup is made by boiling the maple sap in a shallow pan until it contains a high percentage of sugar. When a candy thermometer reads 7° F. above the boiling point of water, the syrup is ready to be strained and bottled. Usually 30 to 40 gallons of sap are required to produce a single gallon of syrup; the amount depends on the sugar content of the sap, which is mostly water.

photo: David Brislance

An Eastern chipmunk out in early March on a lichen-covered log.

In 2011 the first EASTERN CHIPMUNK (left) was spotted in the Waconia area on March 5, and in 2012 one was seen out sunning itself on February 17. These animals are hibernators, yet unlike the thirteen-lined ground squirrels and woodchucks, chipmunks do not put on much pre-hibenation fat, but awaken each week or so during the winter to feed on acorns and other seeds and nuts stored in their underground pantries. They sometimes even emerge during winter warm spells. But we can always expect to see some out in early to mid-March—the beginning of their mating season. The first litter could be born in May and a second in August.

Each male and female constructs and maintains its own burrow, usually in or near woodlands where there are rocky places, stone walls, or a wood pile. Burrows are about two inches wide, have several entrances, and can be as much as ten feet long and five feet deep, with chambers for sleeping, food storage, and waste.

Eastern chipmunks are only active during the day. Although they do climb trees, they spend most of their time on the ground. Adult chipmunks maintain a territory around their burrows, using specific signals to indicate boundaries and avoid combat. Their most common signal is a low bark, the "munk" sound, a single note sometimes repeated over and over for as much as an hour.

Chipmunks make up for their small size with big sounds. When faced with danger, they call "chip, chip, chip," sometimes up to 130 "chips" per minute. In the springtime the "chips" may also serve a social function, as several chipmunks gather to call out their "chips" together.

As with most rodents and other small animals, male chipmunks take no part in raising the young.

Two mallards breaking through the ice in the harbor in Grand Marais.

People living near ponds and lakes have the opportunity to directly observe the SPRING ICE-OUT process, which starts with ice retreating from the shore while the rest of the ice cover turns dark. The main ice sheet weakens and begins to facture in large sections when winds become strong enough to move it. This is followed by rapid melting of ice crystals on the edges of the floating sections as they come into contact with the warmer water. Eventually wind will sweep the last ice sheets from the lake.

As the sheets are pushed ashore, the remaining ice is generally in chunks up to 7 inches thick and honeycomb-shaped. Some loose ice along a shore doesn't constitute the condition of ice still being in, because a boat can easily be pushed through it. I consider ice-out to have occurred when at least 90 percent of the lake is free of ice. Ice-out is an exciting time, as people are anxious to get on the lake. Soon fishing boats, canoes, kayaks, and sailboats will appear and docks will go in, and we're off and running into summer.

MARCH

photos: Jim Gilbert

COMMON SNOWDROPS are the first garden flowers to open each spring. The white blossoms hang downward. Individual flowers are composed of three green-tipped inner petals and three longer, all-white outer petals; the slender leaves grow 3 to 8 inches long. These plants grow best in light shade. Plant bulbs in early fall, spacing them 2 to 4 inches apart and covering them with 2 to 3 inches of soil. Common snowdrops can be left undisturbed for many years. They are natives of Turkey, the Caucasus, and other parts of Europe.

To many gardeners the very name **CROCUS** is a synonym for spring. All crocuses are wildflowers native to the Mediterranean region and into southwest Asia. They send up 1- to 2-inch wineglass-shaped flowers on stems 2 to 6 inches tall before the grass-like leaves are fully developed. Flower colors run through shades of purple, as well as yellow, golden-yellow and white. Many varieties are attractively striped, and all of them have prominent yellow stamens. For the earliest spring bloom, plant crocuses during autumn in a sunny protected spot; for later bloom, plant them on the north side of a hedge or under very light shade. Plant about 2 inches deep. Once planted, crocus bulbs need not be disturbed for years.

GLORY-OF-THE-SNOW is a beautiful plant discovered blooming at the edge of retreating mountain snows in Asia Minor (modern-day Turkey) in the 1800s by a Swiss botanist Pierre-Edmond Boissier. It's a 6-inch gem that bears 8 to 10 violet-blue, white-centered, 1-inch flowers on each stem. Bulbs are planted in early fall 1 to 3 inches apart and covered with 3 inches of soil. Plant in well-drained soil in full sunlight or light shade. Plants bloom in early spring shortly after the first crocus opens. In light shade the flowers will last 3 or 4 weeks. Plants will keep blooming in spring seasons to come, and often sow their own seeds, spreading slowly in a garden.

Waterways start to open up when the average temperature reaches 35° F. for several days running, and the CANADA GEESE follow that 35° isotherm. In southern Minnesota, we look for V formations in early March, and listen for the deep musical honking of the returning geese. They join the wintering-over goose clan whose members then become more active. Canada geese are easily identified by their size—few common birds are larger—and their wingspan, which can extend up to 5½ feet. They are the only geese that have black necks, black heads, and white chin straps. Canada geese mate for life and pairs stay close to each other as much as possible. They start to breed in their third year.

photo: Jim Gilbert

(above) Canada geese, soon after returning, on the edge of Lake Waconia, which was close to losing its ice cover. Ice-out for Lake Waconia was March 18 in 2012—that was 25 days earlier than the average date of April 12.

(below) With melting snow, and before the frost leaves the ground, temporary ponds dot the landscape near Watertown.

photo: David Brislance

A killdeer, an early migrant. We often first hear the bird's flyover cry, "killdeer, killdeer, killdeer" before seeing this welcome harbinger of spring.

photo: Jim Gilbert

photo: Jim Gilbert

A warm, early-March day with south winds brings flocks of male **RED-WINGED BLACKBIRDS** into extreme southern Minnesota. In 2012 this event took place on March 6. There was still snow on the ground, and many of us had thoughts that we could expect more snow and raw winds in the next few weeks. However, the first red-wings were back singing their trilled "o-ka-*leeee*" songs in wetlands, and that was music to our winter-weary ears and a very welcome spring sign. The glossy black males have bright red shoulder patches with a light yellow border. For these males it's serious business to return before the females and stake out claims in marshes and along reedy edges of lakes by singing and flashing red from the tops of the surrounding vegetation, often cattails.

The females arrive several weeks later. They're sparrow-like birds with white eyebrows but otherwise brown above and streaked with brown below. The drab colors will camouflage the female when she sits quietly on her nest.

One of the most widespread and numerous birds in Minnesota, red-wings winter in southern states, sometimes gathering in large flocks along with grackles and cowbirds. But with the first hint of spring, mature males head north. It takes young males two years to become black and to develop the striking red shoulder patches; without the bright colors, the first-year males are unable to win territories or brides and so they gather in flocks and wait for next year. Red-wings feed during the day and rest at night. Their food consists of seeds, berries, insects, and spiders. They walk on the ground when searching for food.

In March we watch for the arrival of the first GREAT BLUE HERONS (right); sometimes they stand on ice-covered lakes. Most of them left in September for places such as south Texas, Mexico, and Central America, with only a very few stragglers seen in the southern part of the state during the winter.

Great blue herons are stately, graceful birds, flying with slow, steady wingbeats, necks drawn in and legs stretched out behind. They stand over three feet tall, with much of their height made up of long legs and a long neck. Their wings measure six feet from tip to tip. Other distinguishing characteristics, aside from the commanding height and blue-gray color, are the largely white neck and head and the six-inch yellow bill.

The great blue heron, or "blue crane" as it is often called, is the largest and best known of American herons. They always return to their breeding range and, specifically, to their nesting rookeries, early in the season. Like most of the heron species, they are very sociable, preferring to nest in congested communities that vary in size from a few pairs to hundreds of birds.

photos: Jim Gilbert

SNOW TRILLIUM (left) is the first to bloom of the woodland wildflowers. They're found in the deciduous woods mostly in the southeastern corner of the state. The snow trillium is the smallest of the trilliums, often blooming in early April, while some remnants of snow remain. The one-inch flowers are made up of three white petals and three green petal-like sepals.

A few **EASTERN BLUEBIRDS** (right) attempt to winter over in Minnesota but nearly all of them spend the cold months in states south of us, returning in greatest numbers between mid-March and mid-April. Their habitat includes farmlands, orchards, roadsides, and open woodlands. They nest in natural tree cavities, old woodpecker holes, wooden fence posts, and the nest boxes we put out for them. Insects make up the main part of their diet, but they also eat fruits and seeds during the months when insects are scarce.

The male bluebird has a sky-blue head, back, and tail, a rusty-red throat and breast, and a white belly; the female is a fainter version of the male. This seven-inch bird is a favorite of many people, but a half-century ago it was nearly eliminated in Minnesota due to the increasing use of insecticides, the dwindling number of wooden fenceposts, and a competition for nest sites from two introduced species—the house sparrow and the European starling. Numerous individuals and organizations have helped bluebirds make a remarkable comeback by establishing and maintaining trails of nesting boxes.

photo: David Brislance

photo: Jim Gilbert

(left) Silver-gray pussy willow catkins. At perfect stage to cut a few twigs to bring indoors for a touch of spring.

photo: David Brislance

A male black-backed woodpecker surrounded by lichens. The black-backed is an uncommon woodpecker of the conifer forests of northeast and north-central Minnesota.

LICHENS can be observed and appreciated at any time of the year, but springtime is when many of these plants are at their colorful best, with rich strong reds, yellows, greens, blues, grays, browns, and blacks. They can be found on the ground, on rocks and on trees, but also on canvas awnings, abandoned cars, and old shoes.

Each lichen is a special organism composed of a fungus and an alga. It's a cooperative venture because algae, which contain chlorophyll, produce all the food for the plants. The fungi repay the algae by providing support—a protective covering. Some lichens look like thick spray paint on a rock surface, others are leaf-like, others bushy, and some hair-like in appearance. Their energy comes from the sun and they collect water and nutrients from the air. For the most part they receive nothing from the surface on which they live except a place to attach and grow.

As a rule, lichens seldom thrive in urban and industrial areas due to atmospheric pollution, so they can be used as indicators of air quality. They can act as pioneers on bare rock or soil, colonizing harsh, inorganic surfaces and preparing areas for mosses, grasses, and trees to follow. Ruby-throated hummingbirds and northern parula warblers use certain lichens for nesting materials. Spruce grouse, moose, white-tailed deer, and flying squirrels dine on lichens as part of their winter food. Lichens have been used for natural dyes and as food in a few cultures. Some may have future value in medicine because of antibacterial or other properties.

Lichens are the dominant vegetation on 8 percent of earth's terrestrial surface. Although about 700 species grow in Minnesota, they're difficult to distinguish from one another, and because they're small they're undoubtedly the most often overlooked component of our landscape.

APRIL

There are many phases to spring each year, but for the sake of simplicity, we could say there are actually two springs. One is the spring of thaw and the other the spring of greening; both can often be found in April.

In a year when spring comes early, the first week of April can bring small green leaves to many types of trees and shrubs; lawns are green and forest floors also begin to "green" up. In a late-spring year, we wait until mid- to late-April to see these things in southern Minnesota, and later in the north.

In April we really *feel* spring—glorious spring, the season of awakening and renewal. Now the greatest show on earth is just outside our windows and backdoors, and everywhere we look. Pasqueflowers bloom on prairies, bloodroots in forests, marsh marigolds in wet spots, and daffodils in our yards. Wood frogs make barking calls, and western chorus frogs, which sound like metallic clickers, are very vocal. Garter snakes and painted turtles come out for some sunning. Great horned owls and bald eagles attend to their nestlings, Canada geese incubate eggs, while American robins and blue jays build nests. As the ice cover retreats from lakes, common loons arrive (in 2012 that happened in March). Gardeners harvest rhubarb and asparagus, start rototilling, and plant onions, potatoes, peas, beets, carrots, lettuce, and radishes. Farmers prepare the soil and some will get early planting done. Minnesota is the nation's fourth-largest corn producer, and farmers like to plant corn by the last week of April or first week of May.

The idea of Earth Day—April 22—is to live in harmony with nature. In April, every forest, marsh, and prairie is full of spring signs—evidence that planet Earth is designed as a place for life, no matter what foolish acts people may commit.

photo: David Brislance

APRIL

The large black and white birds of the lakes, the COMMON LOONS arrive on their spring and summer territories as the ice covers are leaving. Those people in the central and northern part of the state may hear the wild laughing call, "ha-ha-ha-ha," the only call that loons give when they're in flight, perhaps heading for a favorite wilderness lake after wintering along the Gulf Coast. To appreciate loon calls you simply have to hear them in their natural setting. The haunting high yodel call, "oo-AHHH-ho," which we sometimes hear echoing across a lake, is given by the male to announce his claim to territory.

The common loon is Minnesota's state bird and a true symbol of the wildness of our lakes. It prefers clear lakes because it hunts for fish, leeches and other aquatic creatures by eyesight. Swift flights of up to 100 mph take these birds through the air with ease. Not many birds fly faster than loons. When swimming they ride low in the water, and when they dive they can reach depths of 100 feet or more. Males and females look alike.

Ice-out times for lakes here in Minnesota create much interest. It's good to see the blue water and waves, watch the migrating waterfowl, and look for the first common loons out on the lake or the first great blue herons fishing near shore.

The disappearance of the ice is also an event in itself. In the chart below, you can see records for eight of the thousands of lakes that dot Minnesota's landscape, against which to gauge ice-outs on the lakes in your region in years to come.

Lake and County	Ice-Out in 2012	Earliest Ice-Out	Latest Ice-Out	Median Ice-Out (half earlier, half later)	Earliest Record
Lake Pepin Goodhue / Wabasha	March 16	February 29, 2000	May 20, 1843	March 31	1843
Lake Waconia Carver	March 18	March 14, 2000	May 1, 1941	April 10	1940
Lake Minnetonka Hennepin / Carver	March 21	March 11, 1878	May 8, 1856	April 13	1855
White Bear Lake Ramsey / Washington	March 19	March 19, 2012	May 4, 1950	April 14	1928
Lake Minnewaska Pope	March 21	March 21, 2012	May 7, 1950	April 15	1906
Lake Itasca Clearwater	March 26	March 26, 2012	May 18, 1950	April 23	1929
Leech Lake Cass County	April 2	April 2, 2012	May 23, 1950	April 28	1936
Lake Vermilion St. Louis County	April 2	April 2, 2012	May 23, 1950	April 30	1893

photo: Jim Gilbert

photo: Jim Gilbert

Seeing the first TURTLES out sunning is a great spring sign for us, but it must be more thrilling for them, after having spent the winter under the ice. The painted, commonly called a mud turtle, is a small turtle with an upper shell up to 6 inches long and bright orange-red markings on its underside. The painted turtle is the most common of Minnesota's eight turtle species. Ponds and lakes where aquatic vegetation is abundant are their preferred habitat. Their diet consists of about two-thirds water plants and one-third animal food including dead fish, worms, and various aquatic insects.

Although it isn't easy to approach the painted turtle closely, it's probably the least wary of Minnesota turtles. Its habit of sunning just above the water level on a floating log or some other object makes it easy to see. People often wonder why turtles bask in the sunlight with outstretched necks, legs, and tails. Reptile biologists tell us they do this to raise their body temperatures, enabling food to digest. Turtles also receive ultraviolet light for the manufacture of vitamin A. There is no certain evidence that sunning removes parasites.

Flocks of AMERICAN WHITE PELICANS return to many lakes in southern and central Minnesota soon after ice-out. These massive birds have 9-foot wingspans, black flight feathers, and large yellow-orange bills. It's hard to mistake the American white pelican for any other bird.

Early in the breeding season adults develop a raised vertical plate on their bills which is shed later in the year. They can often be seen in flocks soaring high overhead and on lakes where a group may "herd" fish into the shallows.

White pelicans are colonial nesters, preferring remote islands where the entire colony is secure from predators, including humans. They breed regularly on Leech Lake, Marsh Lake in Lac Qui Parle County, Lake of the Woods, and a few other locations in Pope and Faribault Counties.

photo: John Toren

photos: Jim Gilbert

Spring Ephemerals

The **PASQUEFLOWER** is also called prairie crocus or windflower, but the most often used common name in Minnesota is derived from its typical blooming time—the "paschal" season of Easter. This earliest of Minnesota's prairie wildflowers usually blooms in late March into April. It's found in native prairies and on sunny slopes in the south and western parts of the state, as well as in many other parts of western North America and Eurasia. It has become the floral emblem of South Dakota and Manitoba.

The pale purple, 2-inch-wide flowers have 5 to 7 petal-like sepals surrounding a yellow center of stamens with a central tuft of grayish pistils. The entire plant, including the flowers, is covered with silvery soft hairs that may trap warm air during the cool spring season.

One of the earliest plants to appear each year, the handsome **BLOODROOT** emerges from nearly frozen soil, flowering in woodland areas well before trees leaf out. Its nearly 2-inch flowers, each with 8 to 10 white petals and a golden-yellow center, open on sunny days and close again at night. Young leaves unroll in full sunlight, curling up around the flower stalk at night and on cloudy days. After the petals of the flowers have fallen, leaving a pointed seed capsule, the leaf grows much larger and is then one of the most beautiful leaves of the forest.

The name bloodroot is derived not from the root but from the thick, horizontal, underground stem yielding a red-orange juice that has been used by many cultures as a dye and insect repellent.

The **DUTCHMAN'S BREECHES** is a low-growing perennial wildflower of rich woodlands with finely divided leaves in a basal clump and slender arching stems that hold nodding white yellow-tipped flowers drooping in a row. Each flower has two inflated spurs that suggest the legs of tiny trousers, ankles up.

These legs are actually nectar pockets formed by two petals. The delicate flowers are very short lived, so to catch a glimpse of this plant in bloom one has to visit the right habitat often in spring as forest floors are greening up. The plants take advantage of the spring sunshine, before deciduous trees fully leaf out, to make food for their maturing seeds. They also store up some food in underground parts for use the following spring. By mid-summer the leaves have entirely disappeared.

The **WOODCHUCK** is the largest member of the squirrel family in the state. It can weigh up to 14 pounds and measure nearly 2 feet in length. The first ones emerge from hibernation in March, and by April they're commonly seen throughout a good share of Minnesota. Studies suggest that in typical farm country every 6 acres of land has at least one woodchuck. They can live up to about 6 years and spend close to half their life in hibernation.

When woodchucks begin to hibernate in September they're fat. The stored body fat keeps them alive for 6 months, but they lose about 40 percent of their weight before spring, even though their body temperature drops as low as 38 degrees, they take a breath only once every 6 minutes, and their heartbeat drops from 75 to 4 per minute.

Woodchucks are herbivores, feeding on green vegetation and other plant material; they consume as much as a pound of food each day. Favorite foods include grasses, dandelions, plantains, clovers, goldenrods, asters, and some farm-grown food such as alfalfa, peas, corn, and melons. Woodchucks do not eat wood but will climb small trees in spring to eat green buds. They are solitary except for mating and when a mother raises her young.

Individuals have elaborate underground burrows with several exits and chambers. Summer burrows may be 50 feet in length and located in open fields, most often on a hillside or slope. Winter burrows, simpler in structure, are often located at the edge of an open woods or beneath the tangled root system of a tree. About 700 pounds of soil may be removed by a woodchuck while excavating a single burrow system—a process that helps to aerate and mix the soil. Often when areas are burned over, woodchuck burrows save the lives of many animals. Their burrow systems can also provide homes and refuges for skunks, raccoons, foxes, rabbits, weasels, white-footed mice, short-tailed shrews, pheasants, ruffed grouse, and various snakes.

RUBY-CROWNED KINGLET

YELLOW-RUMPED WARBLER

WHITE-THROATED SPARROW

GOLDEN-CROWNED KINGLET

photos: David Brislance

Ruby-crowned Kinglet

A small, 4-inch, green to gray bird with an obvious white eye-ring and one strong white wing-bar, the ruby-crowned kinglet has a characteristic habit of nervously flicking its wings. The male has a ruby crown-patch, which can be hard to see because the bird raises it only for a few seconds when excited. Their song is a long, rich warble, surprisingly loud: *see-see-see-syoo-syoo-syoo-chifferty-chifferty-chifferty*.

Kinglets are among the smallest songbirds. Both species can hover under a branch to glean insects off the undersides of the foliage. The ruby-crowned kinglet is a common spring migrant throughout the state with the bulk of the migration from mid-April to early May. Some kinglets nest in Minnesota's Arrowhead region, though most continue on to Canada's coniferous forests. Most kinglets winter in the southern states, Mexico, and Central America.

White-throated Sparrow

A brown, 6-inch bird with a white throat patch and small yellow dot near each eye, this sparrow is a common to abundant spring migrant throughout the state. They may be encountered in groups ranging from a few birds to hundreds. The peak of migration is from late April into early May. This species nests in the northeast one-third of Minnesota, where its sweet song is a favorite of many people who visit the Boundary Waters Canoe Area. The clear, plaintive, descending song sounds as if the bird is saying, "Old Sam Peabody, Peabody, Peabody," or "Sweet sweet Canada, Canada, Canada." These sparrows are insect, seed, and fruit eaters, and will visit ground feeders where they like cracked corn and millet.

Yellow-rumped Warbler

The yellow-rumped (or myrtle) is our earliest and most abundant spring migrant warbler, sometimes encountered in loose flocks that number into the hundreds of birds. Most of their migration across the state typically occurs from mid-April into early May. Nearly all yellow-rumped warblers winter in the southern states and into Mexico and Central America. They spend summers in the northern coniferous forests over much of Canada and Alaska, though they also nest in Minnesota's Arrowhead country.

The diet of the yellow-rumped warbler consists of insects and berries. Their song is a weak trill, dropping in tone: "tee-tee-tee-brr-brrr." These 5- to 6-inch birds are slate-gray with black streaks on the breast, a white chin and belly, and yellow patches on rump, flanks, and head. Females have duller plumage than males, though the pattern of yellow patches is the same.

Golden-crowned Kinglet

The peak of this diminutive bird's spring migration throughout the state is early to mid-April. In summer this species is a resident primarily in the boreal forests of the north-central and northeastern regions. They winter in southern states and into Mexico and Central America.

This kinglet is 3½ to 4 inches long, olive green above and paler below, with an easy-to-see white wing bar bordered with a black one. The female has a yellow crown, while the male has a orange one, both of them bordered in black. Their song is a series of "seet-seet-seet" notes rising in tone to a tumbling chatter. These birds are insect eaters.

The **SHARP-TAILED GROUSE,** a close relative of the prairie chicken, weighs about two pounds. These birds gather at communal display grounds called leks, generally beginning about mid-March and continuing into May. The males dance in these open areas during courtship, bobbing and strutting while stamping their feet rapidly and inflating sacs of purplish skin on the sides of their necks to produce a booming sound.

A permanent resident in the northern third of Minnesota, this species is most numerous in the northwestern counties. They're usually found in agricultural and prairie grassland bordered by trees, but their populations are fragmented and difficult to locate. Largely vegetarian, the sharptail eats the buds, leaves, and flowers of a variety of plants. The cutting of timber in large areas of northern coniferous forest has created vast tracts of brushland and grassland, actually helping the sharp-tail.

As winter approaches, **AMERICAN TOADS** burrow backward down into the soil to hibernate. With the coming of spring, they dig themselves out of the ground again and head for ponds. Like all amphibians, they must lay their eggs in water.

The male makes his loud, trilling, mating song by puffing out his throat to form a large, sphere-like vocal sac. He then draws air in through his nostrils and passes it repeatedly from lungs to mouth and back again across the vocal chords; the puffed-out throat acts as a resonator.

MARSH MARIGOLDS (right) are members of the buttercup family. They're usually found growing in wet, shallow ditches, quiet lake and pond shores, along streams, and in marshy areas. Plants stand 1 to 2 feet tall; leaves are dark green, broadly heart-shaped, or rounded. The bright yellow flowers, which usually appear from the second week in April into May, provide another sign that the growing season has finally arrived. The abundant blossoms light up the wetlands. The name "marigold" comes from an Anglo-Saxon word meaning "marsh-gold." A second common name for marsh marigold is cowslip and could derive from the fact that this plant grows on hummocks and that cows slipped on it when they went to a stream or pond to drink.

COMPTON'S TORTOISE-SHELL (right) is one of only nine species of Minnesota butterflies that overwinter in the adult stage. Much more common in the north, these lovely creatures can be seen on sunny days when the temperature reaches 50 degrees F. [photo: David Brislance]

In spring the **JAPANESE GARDEN** at the University of Minnesota Landscape Arboretum (opposite page) features the eastern redbud tree. Its purplish-pink, pea-like flowers cover the branches before its leaves appear in the spring. The redbud and other key design elements in the garden draw upon the basics of nature—water, rock, and green plants. Similarly, the garden arbor is built of wood, bamboo, and stone. Pine trees in the half-acre site represent longevity; they've been pruned to look windswept and gnarled, as if they've been in place for hundreds of years.

photos: Jim Gilbert

TULIPS are on display in April at the entrance to the Grace B. Dayton Wildflower Garden at the University of Minnesota Landscape Arboretum. The tulip has been the most popular spring flowering garden plant for centuries; the Dutch have been in the tulip business for more than 400 years. Most tulips have bell-shaped, solitary, single flowers, which come in a wide array of colors from red and pink to white and yellow. Bluish-green leaves rise from the base.

Spring rains leaving a field on a farm tucked into the folds of the Sogn Valley south of Cannon Falls.

Warm temperatures and rain help to continue the growing and greening-up process. Deciduous trees leaf out and produce abundant green tones. Forests are carpeted with blooming wildflowers such as wild blue phlox and cut-leaved toothwort in the south, and trailing arbutus and clintonia in the north, with columbine and large-flowered bellwort throughout the state.

We enjoy the superb fragrances and visual beauty of crab-apple, apple, lilac, and lily-of-the-valley flowers. Corn, spring wheat, potatoes, soybeans, and other crops are planted. Western chorus frogs, spring peepers, leopard frogs, and American toads are vocal. Migrating monarch butterflies arrive. Spring azure and eastern tiger swallowtail butterflies are on the wing. Junebugs (May beetles) hit lighted windows in the evening. Gray squirrel young are out and about.

Mornings offer an avian symphony of bird songs. We're thrilled by the sounds of male red-winged blackbirds trilling, northern cardinals whistling, mourning doves cooing, and the melodious songs of eastern bluebirds, American robins, and white-throated sparrows, even though these songsters are not performing for our benefit. Rose-breasted grosbeaks, Baltimore orioles, and indigo buntings arrive at feeding stations. Look for the first ruby-throated hummingbirds about May 1 in southern Minnesota, and by May 15 in the north. In early May we expect to see newly hatched Canada goose goslings and mallard ducklings; and we watch for chimney swifts and gray catbirds.

By mid-May, typical lake-surface water temperatures are in the 50- to 60-degree range, and the warbler migration is peaking. Late in May, Up North, common loons incubate their eggs, moose

MAY

calves are arriving, black flies can become bothersome, and wild blueberry shrubs have their first white flowers. Throughout the state white-tailed deer are being born; while in the south alfalfa is being cut and gardeners harvest leaf lettuce, radishes, green onions, and the first ripe strawberries.

photo: Jim Gilbert

photo: David Brislance

Equally at home in woodland or water, the gentle **WOOD DUCK** is one of the most beautiful birds in the world. In early May many females are incubating eggs. Serene as this duck appears, it has surprising strength and will come off the water like a rocket when disturbed.

The **BALTIMORE ORIOLES** are back! And these spectacular birds are among those we most eagerly anticipate returning to southern Minnesota yards on or close to May 1 each year. (Others are the chattering house wren, the ruby-throated hummingbird, and the rose-breasted grosbeak.) A fantastic songster, the Baltimore oriole's cheerful series of whistles and chattering is often heard before it's seen. They're easily attracted to feeders offering grape jelly, orange halves, or sugar water. Mix the jelly half-and-half with water using an eggbeater, then pour it into glass jars set out in feeders.

Baltimore orioles are summer residents throughout the state. They feed on insects but also eat wild fruits and may probe flowers for nectar. They winter in Central America.

Flame-orange below and largely black above, the male is very conspicuous as it searches for food. These colors caught the attention of early European settlers in Maryland who named the bird in honor of George Calvert, Lord Baltimore, an early colonizer there; orange and black were his family colors. Females are a paler orange-yellow and brown.

photo: Jim Gilbert

The QUAKING ASPEN, also called trembling aspen and popple, is among the first trees to begin leafing out in the spring. It's the most abundant tree in Minnesota and probably the most widespread native tree in North America. Quaking aspen dot the continent from the treeline in Canada and Alaska south to northern Mexico.

These trees are known for their smooth greenish-white bark, which on older trees becomes brown and furrowed, and their toothed, ovate, simple leaves with petioles (leaf stalks) that are flattened sideways, causing the leaves to quiver in the slightest breeze. This motion intermittently exposes the silvery underside of the leaves—a subtle but beautiful effect. It also makes a sound resembling a light rainfall.

A fast-growing deciduous tree, partly because the bark is also photosynthetic, the quaking aspen is a pioneer, coming in quickly after a fire or logging operation. It has the ability to spread vegetatively by sprouting stems from a shallow root system, a process called root suckering. In this way, a single tree established by one seed can produce hundreds of trees spread over an acre or more. Since all the stems originate from a common root system, they're genetically identical and are considered clones. The root systems that support aspen clones may be the oldest living things on the planet. One in Minnesota has been aged at 8,000 years.

Hundreds of species of insects feed on aspens. The bark is the principal food of the beaver. Porcupines eat the bark and leaves. Black bears find the newly emerged leaves to be a wonderful after-hibernation snack. Ruffed grouse eat the male flower buds in winter. And the quaking aspen also plays a vital role in the paper and chipboard lumber industries.

The **ROSE-BREASTED GROSBEAK** (left) comes to seed feeders in Minnesoa every spring after wintering in locales from Mexico to northern South America. It's a summer resident throughout the state. Its song is like that of an American robin but softer and more melodious.

Both sexes sing. Females are heavily streaked brown-and-white birds with large white eyebrows. Males are black and white with a spectacular triangular rose-red patch in the center of the chest. The name "grosbeak" refers to the bird's large bill, which it uses to crack seeds, although grosbeaks also eat fruit and insects.

The bright, new, lime-green needles and reddish cones of the **NORWAY SPRUCE** are very attractive in early May. Native to northern and central Europe, this tree was introduced into North America by early settlers. It's the largest and fastest growing spruce for landscaping in the North, and is widely used both in shelterbelts and as a larger growing specimen. Mature trees can be up to 90 feet in height and 40 feet in width. The Norway spruce has unique, pendulous (down-hanging) branches and also the largest cone of all the spruces.

photos: Jim Gilbert

(above) Tulip beds in front of the Oswald Visitor Center at the University of Minnesota Landscape Arboretum. (above right) Sandy Gilbert and our dog, Gilbey, in the crabapple collection at the Arboretum. (below right) Common purple lilac.

The **COMMON PURPLE LILAC** is known for its intensely fragrant flowers, borne on 4- to 8-inch long clusters called panicles that usually grow in pairs out from end buds. Many of us have a nostalgic fondness for this shrub, which we associate with a grandmother or mom who picked bouquets and brought them in to let the fragrance permeate the house. Countless cultivars (clones and hybrids) have been developed, so lilacs with white, violet, blue, pink, and purple flowers are now available. My favorite is still the old-fashioned common purple one, which usually blooms in mid-May in central Minnesota. We have seen them blooming as late as early July along the North Shore of Lake Superior.

The common purple lilac shrub (Syringa vulgaris L.) is native to southeastern Europe, but it has been grown in American gardens since early colonial times.

photos: Jim Gilbert

photo: Jim Gilbert

In 2012, the Waconia community, about 30 miles west of downtown Minneapolis, hosted the 2012 Governor's Fishing Opener. Lake Waconia has about 10 miles of shoreline and 3,000 acres of surface area; it's the largest lake in Carver County and the second-largest in the seven-county metropolitan area. (Lake Minnetonka is the largest.) But the people pictured here could be any of the half-million anglers who venture out onto Minnesota lakes for the walleye and northern pike opener each year.

The weather at the governor's event—very light winds, sunny skies, and a high of 72 degrees—made for a pleasant but slow-biting day. Gov. Mark Dayton and thousands of others enjoyed the event, which marks the start of the summer tourism season in Minnesota.

Two of Minnesota's prized catches are the **WALLEYE** and the **NORTHERN PIKE**. The word "walleye" is actually derived from an old Norse word meaning "a light beam in the eye." The walleye's eyes seem to glow because they have a light-sensitive layer of cells which allows the fish to see and feed in the dim light of murky lakes and at dawn and dusk. The walleye also has unusually large, color-sensitive cells. Good eyesight helps these carnivores catch their food, which consists of fish—even other walleyes—leeches, crayfish, and other marine animals.

Some people refer to the walleye as a "pike" but it's actually America's largest perch. Adults range from 2 to 8 pounds, and they never stop growing, so lunkers can reach 15 pounds or more. Long considered to be Minnesota's most popular fish, the walleye became the official state fish in 1965.

The walleye is native to many lakes and streams throughout Minnesota and has also been widely introduced. In fact, walleyes can be found in more than 1,700 lakes in the state and in more than 3,000 miles of river habitat. Its preferred habitat is free of pollution and also provides cover and food, plus rock and gravel spawning shallows. The walleye has a broad distribution in North America from the Northwest Territories east to Labrador and south to North Carolina and Arkansas.

The Northern pike (above) is long and slender, like an aquatic two-by-four; its head is shaped like a duck-bill, with sharp teeth. Northerns often lie in weed beds or by submerged logs waiting for food to come by. Their bodies are built for quick burst of speed, and they'll strike at anything that excites their curiosity, including sunfish, perch, suckers, and even smaller northern pike, plus leeches and frogs, ducklings, small muskrats…or a passing Rapala.

The northern has a greenish body dappled with light spots and a white belly. It's the most widely distributed freshwater fish in the world, being found in North America, Europe, and Asia. It's common in most of Minnesota's lakes and streams. Northerns average 5 to 10 pounds, though individuals weighing more than 45 pounds have been reported.

Like other wild dogs, the RED FOX hunts primarily at night. Most often alone much of the year, they sleep curled up in a ball at the base of a tree or rock, even in winter. They are found throughout Minnesota, but their range includes North America and Eurasia, where they live in a variety of habitats from arctic to temperate zones.

Red foxes especially like countrysides where there are mixed woodlands and fields. Because much farmland is like this they are frequently found in rural areas dotted with farms. They mate between January and March, and the females typically bear four to six kits in April or May, after a 51- to 53-day gestation.

The male and female, both monogamous, stay with each other from the breeding season until the young are dispersed, usually at the end of September.

The den is only occupied for birthing and raising young. It consists of a burrow that the foxes dig themselves or remodel from the den of another animal. While the mother stays with the young in the den, the father hunts for his family, bringing back mice, voles, rabbits, squirrels, and birds. Red foxes are omnivores, so they also eat berries, other fruits and nuts, plus fish, insects, and carrion.

Adult red foxes weigh 7 to 15 pounds, are about 3 feet long, including the large bushy tail with the white tip, and stand about 15 inches tall. They are normally rusty red with black legs and white chest and belly. A few red foxes are black or silver and others are "cross" foxes—brownish with a cross-shaped darker area over the shoulders. These are genetic variants and may occur in otherwise typical litters.

Previous page: Red fox and kits, near Isabella, Minnesota, May 14, 2012. [photo: David Brislance]

The LARGE-FLOWERED TRILLIUM is found throughout much of the eastern half of the United States, in rich moist deciduous woodlands, and is abundant in Minnesota

except in the northeastern and southwestern corners. It carpets vast areas with green and white, frequently growing in colonies in open or deep shade. The single white 2- to 4-inch flowers with yellow anthers are quite long-lasting and turn pink with age. Three broad leaves, plus three flower petals and three pointed green petal-like sepals mark the trilliums. The famous Swedish botanist, Carl Linnaeus (1707–1778) coined the name "trillium" to describe the plant's "threeness." The large-flowered trillium stands 12 to 18 inches tall and blooms at the time tree leaves are emerging and growing to full size.

JACK-IN-THE-PULPIT is a stately but strange-looking spring wildflower found in rich, moist, deciduous woods. It stands 15 to 30 inches tall. Look for thrice-parted leaves, and at the top of a single stalk a flower made up of "Jack" or the preacher in a canopied pulpit. "Jack" is the spadix— this stick-like, flower-bearing club actually has the tiny male or female flowers at its base. The flap-like spathe is green

or purplish-brown, often striped, and curves gracefully over "Jack." In August and September female plants can produce clusters of bright red berries.

MAY

photos: Jim Gilbert

One of 42 species of native Minnesota orchids, we can expect to find the LARGE YELLOW LADY'S-SLIPPER growing in wet, shady, deciduous woods or swamps and bogs at the time when tree leaves are close to full-size. They can be seen throughout the state, except in the southwestern corner. The plants are 10 to 20 inches tall, have leafy stems, and bear one or two flowers, each about 2 to 3 inches in size. The flowers resemble clear yellow pouches or slippers with brown twisted frills or ties on either side.

Enjoy large yellow lady's-slippers in the wild as they are nearly impossible to transplant. Orchids are highly specialized plants that require their own special fungus growing on their roots to survive.

Found throughout Minnesota, COLUMBINE grows 2 to 3 feet tall, has leaflets with three lobes, and drooping red and yellow flowers from May into June. The nectar tubes extending upward make it a favorite flower of hummingbirds and long-tongued moths.

In rocky terrain wild columbine is seen growing at odd angles, sometimes precariously perched among the rocks where soil is scarce, but its roots reach deep into the earth. It is also found along roadsides and forest borders. Our native columbine is an easy wildflower to grow and one of outstanding beauty. Seeds sown in a garden produce seedling that bloom in the second year. Collect seeds only; don't dig up the plants. Later in summer, the papery pod-like fruit splits along its side to release many shiny round seeds.

Botanists have identified an estimated 22,000 different orchid species growing everywhere from the arctic tundra to the steamy tropics. In Minnesota we have 42 species. One of the largest orchids here, and the only lady's-slipper with no leaves on the stem, is the MOCCASIN-FLOWER, also called the pink lady's-slipper.

What a commanding presence it is. Decades ago I found my first one blooming in a jack pine forest near Itasca State Park in early summer. I will never forget that experience.

Known flowering dates range from late May into early July. The plants have two parallel-veined basal leaves, a long stem with a single, two-inch-long, deep rose-red flower with four brownish frills, and are 6 to 18 inches tall. Most often found in the northern half of Minnesota (except in the western counties) the moccasin-flower is certainly the most frequently seen lady's-slipper. It grows in a wide variety of forest habitats from dry sandy pine forests to the wettest coniferous bogs. The main requirements are shade and an acid soil.

The dust-like seeds of the moccasin-flower may remain dormant for several years until they hook up with the right soil fungus, allowing them to germinate—the chances are one in several hundred thousand. Following germination the tiny plant develops underground. During the third or fourth year after germination, the plant may send up its first green leaf, and sometime after the eighth year it will produce its first flower. Once established, it's possible that a plant may bloom for a hunded consecutive years or more. Do not attempt to transplant a moccasin-flower.

Spring Warblers

Small, active birds that often hide in the foliage, warblers go unnoticed by many people. However, most experienced birders love the warblers and look forward to their spring arrival as one of the highlights of the year. On a single day between about May 12 and 20, if conditions are right, 15 or 20 species of these little migrating songsters can be observed.

Most warblers winter in the tropics, from Mexico and the Caribbean to South America. These warm-weather birds feed mainly on minute insects, coming into Minnesota and places farther north for the nesting season. Although a good share of the warblers are brightly patterned and flit about in trees, some have more solid colors and work closer to or on the ground.

The **CAPE MAY WARBLER** (above left) summers in the northern spruce forest and winters mostly on Caribbean islands. Adult males are striking, with black stripes on a yellow breast, a rich chestnut ear patch, and a yellow neck. Females are similar but duller and without the ear patch.

The lively, buzzy song—*zee,zee,zee,zoo,***zee***—of the **BLACK-THROATED GREEN WARBLER** (below left) is often heard in late spring and through much of the summer in the coniferous and mixed forests of the northeast and north-central regions of Minnesota, as he engages in territorial conversation with his neighbors. The "boot greens," as these birds are affectionately called, have yellow faces, black throats, and moss-green backs and crowns.

Always a pleasant surprise at a feeding station, **INDIGO BUNTINGS** have usually returned to Minnesota from their winter homes by mid-May. They nest throughout the state in rural roadside thickets and where woodlands meet open areas. Like many other bird species, the indigo bunting is a boon to farmers and fruit growers, consuming insect pests and weed seeds. Females are light brown with faint markings. Males appear a vibrant blue, though their feathers are actually black. As with blue jays, sunlight is refracted within the structure of the indigo bunting's feathers, giving them their dazzling, iridescent color.

photos: David Brislance

This newly-born **WHITE-TAILED DEER** was photographed on May 22, 2012, in Cook County. Most fawns are born in late May and early June after a gestation period of 196 to 213 days. At birth they weigh about 7 pounds.

Found in the wooded parts of the state, the **SCARLET TANAGER** (left) is a tropical-looking bird that hunts for insects high in the tops of trees. The male is bright red with black wings and tail; the female is a drab greenish-yellow bird with olive wings and tail. These birds winter in South America.

MAY

On the first day of June summer arrives, according to meteorologists, who remind us that this day marks the beginning of what is historically the warmest 92 days of the year.

We all can feel that the pace of life has slowed down a bit. June 1 brings with it the sense of completion. Yes, the school year is over, or nearly so—the same with graduations. At the same time, woodlands are also thick with lush new leaves, the migrating birds have returned, and the daylight hours are long. Let summer begin!

The sun is high in the sky in June and each acre of land here in the Upper Midwest is receiving more radiant energy than in equatorial South America or Africa. We can soon expect lakes to be in the 70s and perfect for swimming. The long hours of sunlight promote nesting behavior in birds, including the Baltimore orioles, purple martins, tree swallows, and warblers.

The insects and plants also respond to the long daylight. Deer flies and stable flies, luna moths and fireflies take flight. Meanwhile, our Minnesota state floral emblem, the showy pink and white lady's-slipper, blooms elegantly, and common milkweed has clusters of fragrant flowers. Blooming northern catalpa trees and Japanese tree lilacs, along with peonies and garden roses, add much color to our yards. Farmers cultivate corn and soybeans, and gardeners pick buckets of ripe strawberries.

JUNE

Rapid heating of the air just above ground can clash with cold air aloft, creating thunderheads, which makes June traditionally the wettest and most tornado-prone month of the year. So keep an eye on the sky while you enjoy the long, warm days of June, full of nature's wonders.

photos: David Brislance

photo: David Brislance

This photo shows the rare spreading pose of a male EASTERN TAILED BLUE BUTTERFLY on blooming bunchberry at Lutsen. Males are blue with black borders on all wings. Females are only slightly blue. This tiny creature (one-inch wingspan) can be found along roadsides and in forest clearings and old fields. Both sexes are light gray-white below with black spots and two bigger orange spots near the tail. Three broods each year are possible; the flight period is from mid-May into September. The caterpillars feed on flowers and buds of legumes such as vetches and clovers. Adults sip nectar from wildflowers such as wild strawberry, clovers, asters, and goldenrods.

RUBY-THROATED HUMMINGBIRDS are a joy to watch. These tiny birds burn up so much energy they're forced to eat almost constantly, and keep right on feeding into twilight after most other birds have begun roosting for the night. The bird's appearance is unmistakable—metallic green above and white below. It gets its name from the ruby throat of the male (below), which actually looks black in many lights. It's Minnesota's smallest bird and the only hummingbird that nests here.

Survival for a hummingbird depends on fast movements, and courage. They can hover, move backwards, and dart forward at high speed to outmaneuver other birds. Being aggressive in defense of territory, they will go after much larger birds such as crows and blue jays, using their long needle-sharp bill as a dagger.

Ferns are a conspicuous part of Minnesota's natural vegetation except in the prairie region of the western edges. The state's list of native ferns includes 47 species. While trees seek light, ferns thrive best in cool, moist, shaded forest places. In the northeastern and southeastern part of the state, the ferns are the most abundant part of the ground cover. The rootstocks of ferns grow on or just below the ground.

Each spring one of the earliest ferns to send up fiddleheads that become new leaves is the coarse, rugged INTERRUPTED FERN (below). Interrupted fern fronds are, in fact, interrupted by one to five pairs of short stalks laden with round, green-to-brown spore cases located about two-thirds of the way up the frond and easily spotted at a glance. Even after the spores are dispersed and the cases disintegrate, the frond is still left with a noticeable gap. Fronds easily reach 3 to 4 feet.

photo: David Brislance

photo: Jim Gilbert

The NORTHERN PARULA is a small, 4½-inch warbler that most often keeps to the treetops. Its distinctive, sputtering, buzzy song, "zz-zz-zzz-zzzeeee-wup," is sometimes compared to a high-pitched ascending ratchet. The bird is more often heard than seen. They are blue-gray above, with a yellow-green "saddle" on the back, white wing-bars, yellow on the throat and breast, and a white belly. Males have black and rusty chest bands. Northern parulas are summer residents in northeastern and north-central Minnesota where they hide their nests in usnea (beard lichen). They winter from Mexico to Nicaragua.

JUNE

photos: Jim Gilbert

The Sawtooth Mountains as seen from Artist's Point in Grand Marais.

The **BIRD'S-EYE PRIMROSE** and the star-shaped, shiny leaves of the **BUTTERWORT** are both found in the hostile environment of the "splash zone" of Lake Superior's shore. Bird's-eye primrose grows on rock ledges. Its seemingly fragile flowers, atop narrow stems, can be found from late May through June rising ftom crevices in the volcanic rock.

photos: David Brislance

MONARCH BUTTERFLIES (above) on blooming pin cherry trees near Grand Marais, June 1, 2012. When conditions are right, late in May or early in June, hundreds of these 4-inch butterflies can be seen nectaring on flowering trees and other plants. Monarchs are bright burnt-orange with black veins and black margins speckled with white dotes. The caterpillars feed on milkweed, dogbane, and related plants. One of the most common and easily recognized butterflies, the monarch is the only butterfly that annually migrates both north and south the way birds do. Monarchs from Minnesota winter in the fir forests of mountainous middle Mexico.

PURPLE CLEMATIS (left) blooming at Lutsen—a rather scarce native vine of rocky woods, climbing by tendrils. The bell-like flowers never open fully.

photo: Jim Gilbert

The **Luna moth** has a wingspan of 4 inches. Each wing has a prominent eyespot; the tops of the front wings are edged with purple, and the hind wings end in long ribbon tails. During the daytime the moth hangs in the foliage of trees, and those long projections of the hind wings, folded together, resemble a leaf stem, camouflaging it from predators while it rests. Found only in North America, the luna moth is seen from late May to late June in Minnesota. They can be encountered near porch lights in the morning, if the lights have been on during the night, and on streetlight posts.

In early June of 2012 I saw lunas in both southern and northern Minnesota. On June 2, I spotted two mating pairs just a few yards apart on the ridge above Lake Superior.

The luna lays eggs that are cemented to twigs and leaves of its favorite food plants—birch, aspen, and willow. All summer the green caterpillars grow as they eat the leaves, and in the fall they spin cocoons of their abundant silk among the leaf litter where they'll spend the winter. Luna moths live on the leaf energy the caterpillars stored the previous summer. The adult moths don't have mouths or stomachs. They mate, the females deposit eggs, and they die, usually in less than a week.

photos: David Brislance

A CANADIAN TIGER SWALLOWTAIL (above) rests on moose maple at Lutsen. There is only one brood each summer; the flight period is from late May into July.

A TWELVE-SPOTTED SKIMMER on blossoms of WILD LUPINE. This stunning, two-inch dragonfly has 12 black spots and 10 white spots on its wings. You can see them flying from May through September.

Wild lupine is native to the western states, but has also become a popular garden plant in the East, where it escapes from gardens and now puts on a show in June along roadsides and other sunny locations. These plants are especially numerous in northeastern Minnesota, where they crowd out native wildflowers. Lupine flowers can be white, pink, blue, or purple, purple being the most common.

The GRAY TREEFROG (right) is also called the common tree frog. This 1- to 2-inch green frog with a white belly can switch color to gray accompanied by dark spots, as the temperature, humidity, or habitat changes.

They are found in a variety of woodland habitats throughout Minnesota except in the southwest. Males are very vocal in June with their melodic trills. These small insect-eaters have toe pads and produce a sticky substance that allows them to climb smooth surfaces such as window panes without difficulty.

photos: David Brislance

A **WHITE-THROATED SPARROW** fledgling (above) waiting for the return of a caring parent in Superior National Forest.

A male **CHESTNUT-SIDED WARBLER** (left) with his new fledglings, in Superior National Forest. This warbler species is a summer resident in northern Minnesota; it winters from Nicaragua to Panama. The sexes are similar, featuring a yellow-green crown, a wide chestnut line on the sides, and white underparts. The attractive 5-inch bird has a rich musical song, which is sometimes interpreted as "very , very pleased to MEET-CHA." They typically build their nests only two feet off the ground in small shrubs, and lay four eggs, which the female incubates for 11 or 12 days.

photo: David Brislance

A BLACK-CAPPED CHICKADEE feeds its fledgling. This bird calls its own name: "chick-a-dee-dee-dee." The clear, whistled "fee-bee," the second note lower, is considered the chickadee's true song, and can be heard in any month of the year, but most frequently in spring when the nesting season approaches.

These birds are found throughout Minnesota and readily come to feeding stations. Both sexes work hard to excavate a cavity in the rotting wood of a tree trunk or dead branch where a nest will be built. That's quite a job for these 5-inch birds. They will also nest in abandoned woodpecker holes and in nesting boxes. Usually 6 to 8 eggs are laid; incubation is by the female alone and lasts 12 to 13 days. The male feeds his mate on the nest and helps care for the young.

photos: Jim Gilbert

SHRUB ROSES (above) at the University of Minnesota Landscape Arboretum. June is rose month, when we can see the most blossoms from the many types of roses. It's the combination of elegance and charm that has made roses as a group the best-known and most popular ornamental plant in the world.

SHOWY PINK AND WHITE LADY'S-SLIPPER (right) at the U of M Landscape Arboretum. The official state flower of Minnesota, it's the largest and most impressive orchid found in the state. It blooms at the same time as Russian olive trees and double peonies.

photo: David Brislance

An **ATLANTIS FRITILLARY BUTTERFLY** on a northern bush-honeysuckle, Lutsen. With a wingspan of about 2½ inches, Atlantis is a medium-sized fritillary. It's also the most northern of the fritillaries. There is one brood each summer; the flight period is from late June through August. These butterflies winter in the caterpillar stage which feeds on violets. The orange and black adults nectar on fireweed, the hawkweeds, and a variety of other wildflowers.

Blooming **PEONY** (right) in the Terrace Garden at the University of Minnesota Landscape Arboretum.

photo: Jim Gilbert

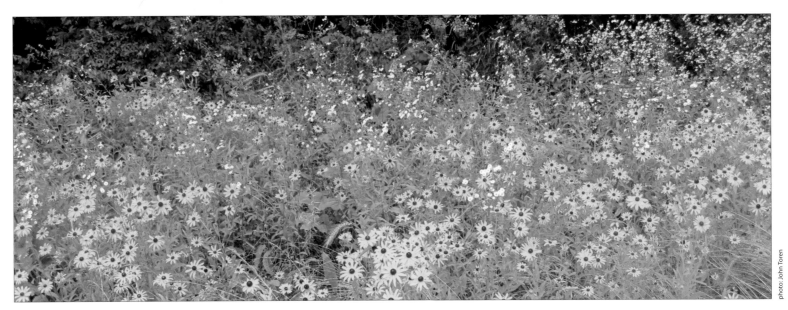

Roadside wildflowers near Preston, Minnesota.

Records show that July is normally Minnesota's warmest and sunniest month, heating the lakes up for the best swimming conditions and allowing corn to grow tall. On average, the peak of the summer heat occurs around July 26. During the month farmers harvest small grains; gardeners pick cucumbers, zucchini, and tomatoes; young Canada geese test their new flight feathers; and wild bumble bees continue their important pollination work. From the filtered light of the forest comes the plaintive "pee-a-wee" call of the eastern wood-pewee, and the short, insistent, robin-like phrases of the red-eyed vireo, repeated endlessly.

In the first week of July, in southern Minnesota, garden raspberry picking is good, the first full-sized tomatoes are ripe, and the first new potatoes are dug. Giant sunflowers are starting to bloom, field corn is usually up 4 to 6 feet, and soybeans begin blooming.

By the Fourth of July, butternut trees may begin to show a few yellow leaflets—an early fall sign as one season slides slowly into the next. From the Iowa border north to Canada, expect to see fireflies helping light up the countryside on these warm nights.

During the second week of July, shorebirds such as lesser yellowlegs and least sandpipers often begin to appear, having begun their long trek from the arctic. They are probably adults that were unsuccessful in nesting, but this still marks the beginning of fall migration. Prairies at this time offer the most conspicuous wildflowers. Red mulberry and wild blackcap raspberry fruit is ripe and good eating. In southwest and western Minnesota, and on into the Dakotas, the combining of wheat begins. In northern Minnesota, firewood has radiant flowers and dragonflies are numerous.

During the third week in July we often enjoy our first meals of

JULY

locally grown sweet corn. Garden perennials in bloom include day-lilies and hollyhocks. Many pollinating cornfields are seen. Canada geese begin flying again. On hot days, male annual cicadas keep buzzing until about 30 minutes after sunset.

Most Minnesota lakes will rise to 80 degrees or warmer on the surface during the last week in July. Wild chokecherry fruit is ripe; these cherries are popular for jelly making and very important as food for wildlife. Purple martins are observed in flocks, already staging for migration. Wild serviceberries, blueberries, pin cherries, and red raspberries are ripe in northern Minnesota.

The **American goldfinch** (above right) is a widespread resident throughout most of Minnesota. In summer the male is bright yellow with black forehead, wings, and tail; the females are a duller but still-attractive yellow-green. Winter birds vary from yellowish-brown to gray. Goldfinches often travel about in flocks; their undulating flight and twittering "potato-chip, potato-chip" call is hard to miss. These 5-inch birds visit feeders for sunflower and thistle seeds. Because they nest so late, they raise only a single brood each year. Gold-finches feed heavily on wild thistle seeds and line their nests with thistle down. They are the only songbirds that feed their young a diet of seeds.

The **Western prickly pear cactus** (below right) is one of two species of cacti occurring in the state. It's native to south-western Minnesota where it's found on prairies and other dry rocky places. The leaves are flat, fleshy, green pads covered with tufts of sharp spines. Usually from late June into July, the 2- to 3-inch yellow flowers appear, followed by round edible fruits that start out green and later turn purple. Flower flies, bees, and other insects often visit the pollen-rich flowers.

JULY

photo: David Brislance

Among hummingbird species, only the **RUBY-THROATED HUMMINGBIRD** nests east of the Rocky Mountains. This species is a summer resident in Minnesota. Banding records tell us that the hummingbirds we see in our yards may well return next summer, and perhaps for several more. The tiny ruby-throats are only about 3 inches long, with an average weight of 3.4 grams. It would take about 130 of these birds together to weigh 1 pound. Their top flight speed is just under 30 mph.

Many of us put out sugar-water feeders, with a mixture of one part white sugar to four parts water, to lure these gems of the bird world close enough so we can hear the humming sound from their rapid wing beats. However, few of us ever find a nest, much less a nest in active use like the one pictured above.

During courtship, the female ruby-throat sits quietly on a perch while the male displays in a pendulum dance. He flies in a wide arc and buzzes loudly with each dip, but the female shows no preference for a particular male until just prior to egg laying. Observers agree that the male takes no part in nesting activities and is even suspected of polygamy. Occasionally a male may be seen near the nest, but after mating, he apparently becomes a free wanderer. He spends his time perched on a twig, resting and preening, while his mate chooses a nesting site, builds the nest, and rears the brood.

When she is building a nest, she chooses a limb or twig, often one positioned 10 to 20 feet off the ground and sheltered by overshadowing leaves. She then collects silky or downy fibers and binds them together with spider silk. The nest, 2 inches or less in diameter, is then covered with bits of lichen.

Nest building takes about a week. The finished nest looks like a small knot covered with tree lichens. The two white eggs, laid one day apart, are about the size of large peas. The female incubates the eggs, which hatch in 14 days.

The new-born young stay in the nest for about 20 days. Fledglings stay with their mother for another week or so. Nesting takes place from June into July; only one brood is raised each year.

We usually pick the first ripe GARDEN RASPBERRIES on July 1 in the Twin Cities area, but in 2012 it was on June 12. Because raspberries are quite fragile and perishable, making it difficult to market them widely, they're especially valuable as a home garden fruit. They're easy to grow if you have a sunny location. And here in Minnesota the wild red raspberry is also one of the most common shrubs, especially in the northern two-thirds of the state, giving outdoor adventurers the chance to pick this great tasting fruit out in the field.

Red raspberries are about 84 percent water but they also contain vitamins A and C, along with minerals, including potassium. The raspberry fruit is an aggregate—each of the little bumps in the berry is a tiny fruit itself, complete with a seed and fleshy covering. The berries should be picked as soon as they can be easily slipped off the core without breaking the texture of the berry.

The English name raspberry comes from the thorny canes that will *rasp* your legs when you walk through a thicket of them.

True LILIES like the ones pictured above, from the University of Minnesota Landscape Arboretum, are members of the genus Lilium. They're distributed across temperate regions worldwide, with the greatest numbers being found wild in eastern Asia. Minnesota has two native lilies, both with orange flowers. Over long periods of time gardeners and botanists have developed many hybrids which are sold as named cultivars such as "Connecticut King" and "Orange Light."

Lilies are among the finest of the summer-blooming bulbs. Each leafy stem is terminated by a cluster of showy flowers; white, yellow, orange, red, and purple are the common colors. Lilies can be grown in rows for cut flowers or combined with other perennials in a garden. By selecting species and cultivars with different flowering dates, continuous bloom can be obtained from early June until mid-September. The best overall bloom is expected soon after the Fourth of July.

Mid-Summer Flowers

photos: Jim Gilbert

The **CLEMATIS** (right) gets its name from the Greek word "klematis," meaning a kind of vine. These purple-flowered cultivars are growing on a trellis at the U of M's Landscape Arboretum. These climbing garden perennials grow upward by twisting their leaf stalks around their support, and are known for their showy large flowers, which come in a diverse array of colors. We have two native clematis species in Minnesota, both with relatively small flowers.

The **TAWNY DAYLILY** is native to Europe and Asia but has long since become naturalized in the eastern United States, including Minnesota. The orange-red flowers are about 5 inches long and 4 inches across. This plant blooms from mid-June through July and into August and is common in gardens and along alleyways. Like other daylilies, the tawny daylily has long, strap-shaped leaves and tall leafless flowering stems. Individual flowers last only one day although the plants produce a succession of bloom for several weeks. There are hundreds of cultivars for gardeners to choose from, ranging from yellow and orange to red and maroon. Each flower has six stamens, three petals, and three petal-like sepals. The plants require hot days to put on their best show. In fact, daylilies withstand heat and drought better than most garden flowers, and are considered the most reliable of summer-flowering perennials.

The **DELPHINIUM** (above) is a tall, dignified, garden perennial that likes sunny locations. The stately 4- to 6-foot, blue-flowered plants are impressive when grouped in perennial borders. Delphiniums thrive best where summers are cool. Their chief flowering time is in June and July, but if the main spike is cut off when the flowers have faded, smaller, secondary shoots will extend the blooming season. The original species, or wild types, from which the modern varieties have come, are natives of California, Siberia, India, and other locations.

Here Sandy Gilbert admires the delphiniums in one of the gardens at Glensheen in Duluth.

The **OVENBIRD** (left) sings "Teacher! Teacher! Teacher!" Maybe it's because I'm a teacher that this warbler's song appeals to me. Although the song is loud and easy to recognize, this earth-colored, insect-eating bird can be very difficult to spot, as they spend much of their time on the leafy forest floor. The handsome ovenbird has an orange crown, white eye ring, striped chest, and olive-brown back. Males and females look alike and retain their coloration all year. This rather large 6-inch warbler gets its name from the nest it builds on the ground in the shape of a domed outdoor oven.

Ovenbirds are summer residents throughout the wooded portions of the state, mainly in the northern, east-central, and southeastern regions. They winter from the Gulf of Mexico to northern South America.

A male **MOURNING WARBLER** (below left) in Cook County. The mourning warbler is a summer resident throughout the wooded portions of the north-central and northeastern one-third of the state. They are hard to find and even harder to photograph because they hang out in dense cover close to the ground. Adult males are olive above, yellow below, with a gray hood (the "mourning" shroud) and a patch of black on the lower throat. Females are paler. These intriguing 5-inch birds are insect eaters. Their nests are built on or near the ground in jewelweed, ferns, grass tussocks, or prickle plants. They winter from Nicaragua to northern South America.

This recently fledged **MERLIN** (right), a mid-sized falcon, was photographed in Cook County. They're a scarce summer resident of northern Minnesota, although since the 1980s they've begun to nest more frequently in cities and towns along the North Shore of Lake Superior. Formerly known as the "pigeon hawk," merlins are renowned for chasing down birds from chickadee to jay size in fast, swooping flights.

photos: David Brislance

87

In Minnesota, CORN is an annual, usually planted in May. Various varieties of sweet corn are harvested from July into September, with the main harvest time for field corn varieties stretching from late September through November.

Corn is a grass domesticated centuries ago by indigenous people in Mexico and Central America. The Aztec and Mayan people cultivated numerous varieties. Today 350 types are grown in Peru, and in the United States corn is the number one agricultural crop in both volume and value. Minnesota is fourth in the nation in corn production, following Iowa, Illinois, and Nebraska.

An average ear of corn typically has 800 kernels in 16 rows. That's pretty amazing when you think of one seed being turned into 800, and sometimes more than one ear is produced on a single plant. Just think of the many uses and countless products coming from corn, including plastics, ethanol, cooking oil, corn syrup, and popcorn. But also ponder the pollination biology that makes it all possible. The tassels on top of the plants function to produce ample quantities of pollen to fertilize the female structures—the "ears." The tassels normally emerge a day or so before the first silks appear.

Each silk is a long slender tube attached to the potential kernel on the ear. (A pollen grain must slide down each tube to fertilize the egg and begin developing a kernel.) It's a mind-boggling process.

(above) Tassels, the male structures of corn. They produce great quantities of pollen.
(below right) Silks catch pollen and send their nuclei to the corn ear, the female flowering structure. There is one silk for each kernel of corn on a cob.

(below left) A cornfield near Waconia.

photos: Jim Gilbert

photo: John Toren

Ripe and ripening BLUEBERRIES. As I write this entry on June 19, 2012, 1 have just come inside after eating a couple of handfuls of the first ripe garden blueberries. Yes, they were delicious. Not only do blueberries, with their 83 percent water content, taste great, but they're valuable for the nutrients they contain, including vitamins A and C, calcium, phosphorus, potassium, and some of the B vitamins. Over the years I've picked and eaten wild blueberries across scattered parts of northern Minnesota from late June to late September.

Botanically, the blueberry, like the currant, gooseberry, grape, and tomato, is a true berry—a fleshy fruit usually containing many seeds. Blueberries have small, soft seeds, are juicy and sweet, and exhibit a distinct taste. Many American Indian tribes ate them both fresh and dried. Blueberry fruit is also important to American wildlife such as grouse, scarlet tanagers, thrushes, chipmunks, and black bears.

photo: Jim Gilbert

Cook County Denizens

A BULL MOOSE (left), on July 12, 2008. About the size of a horse, and weighing more than a thousand pounds, the moose is our largest wild animal. The same species found in northern Minnesota also roams the boreal forests of Eurasia. An extremely quiet animal while feeding in the woods, they are able to eat up to 45 pounds of vegetation per day. They spend lots of time in the water during the summer, keeping cool, eating aquatic plants, and avoiding biting insects. Moose swim well and feed on submerged as well as surface aquatics. Bulls begin to grow new antlers in April; the velvet is lost in August, and the antlers are shed in winter.

[photo: David Brislance]

This NORTHERN PARULA WARBLER chick (right above) left its nest on July 28, 2010. Breeding mostly in coniferous forests of the North, this species prefers beard lichen for nest sites. Commonly 4 or 5 eggs are laid in a basket-shaped nest built of fine grasses and well hidden in lichen strands.

A GRAY FOX kit (right) in mid-July. The gray fox prefers the wooded areas of the state. It's sometimes called the tree fox, and probably climbs to escape large predators more than to find food. One litter per year is produced, averaging 4 young. Thought to mate for life, a pair will defend a territory of 2 to 3 square miles. Related to dogs and wolves, the gray fox only weighs 7 to 13 pounds, is mostly nocturnal, and feeds on small animals and various fruits.

photos: David Brislance

photo: Jim Gilbert

A CHIPPING SPARROW (right), spotted on July 20, 2010, near Lutsen. A familiar songbird, the chipping sparrow is a common summer resident throughout the state. It's found in both urban and rural areas, and especially in the heavily forested areas in the north. In our yards they are often seen feeding on dropped seeds below feeders. Their food consists mainly of seeds, but in summer the adults and young also feed on insects. They raise two broods of young each year, and then head south to winter in southern states, Mexico, and Central America.

The common name, chipping sparrow, comes from the song, a rapid musical trill on a single pitch. Males and females look alike. These 5-inch birds are streaked with brown above, are clear gray below, have a rusty-brown cap, and a black line through the eye. [photo: David Brislance]

A warm end-of-July day on Lake Waconia, with water temperature close to 80 degrees—the Gilbert grandkids (Lukas, Ailsa, Anja, and Lonne) are ready for swimming.

Walking the dog on a misty July morning in the bluff country near the Iowa-Minnesota border.

photo: John Toren

photo: John Toren

A bright August morning on the Vermilion River south of the Canadian border near Crane Lake.

August usually lacks the extreme heat of July. The Atlantic high pressure system dominates the region, bringing us mostly sunny skies and light winds. Canoe trips, tubing in streams, swimming, and pontoon-boat excursions are all enhanced by the warm water conditions. Early-season varieties of Minnesota apples are ripe throughout the month. We feast on sweet corn and garden-ripe tomatoes, listen to the shrill buzzing of annual cicadas announcing the heated air, and watch swallows and monarch butterflies stage for migration. Summer still rules but many shorebirds move southward and touches of autumn colors begin to appear. The wetlands are filled with showy blooming wildflowers including jewelweed, blue vervain, boneset, and Joe-Pye weed.

In early August, some birds are still singing, including mourning doves, cardinals, purple martins, and catbirds. It's American goldfinch nesting time, now that thistle seeds are ripe. Ruby-throated hummingbirds are more numerous, so put up another feeder. Ragweeds, both great and common, begin shedding pollen into the air. These ragweeds probably account for more hay fever symptoms than all other Minnesota plants combined.

The first ripe muskmelons and honeydew melons are ready to pick. Gladiolus flowers are showy in gardens, and hosta flowers are visited by bumble bees and hummingbirds. Beekeepers begin extracting honey. The third crop of alfalfa is being harvested, and soybean fields have new pods. Ripe wild grapes can be used for snacks: dozens of bird species relish this fruit. In northern Minnesota, blueberry picking is good in many jack pine forests; and evening primrose, pearly everlasting, and fireweed are among the showy plants blooming along the roadside.

The second half of August is also full of nature's happenings. Snapping turtle eggs are hatching. Spider webs glisten with dew.

AUGUST

Nests of the bald-faced hornet—the original paper-maker—grow, layer by layer; they look like gray footballs hanging up in the trees. Evenings resound with the sleigh-bell chirping of snowy tree crickets. Monarch butterflies have begun aggregating, the beginning stage of migration, and some are already heading south. Migrating birds include common nighthawks, purple martins, and various "confusing" fall warblers. White-tailed deer fawns have grown and are losing their spots. Many asters and goldenrods are blooming, and purple and golden-yellow now dominate the woodland borders. Mushrooms appear like magic in moist woods.

RED-BREASTED NUTHATCHES are permanent residents in the northeastern and north-central parts of the state, and are winter visitors in the south. These small, 4½-inch birds have gray backs, a prominent eye line, and a rusty-red breast and belly. Males display a black cap and females a gray cap. The name "nuthatch" comes from a Middle English nickname "nuthak," referring to the habit of wedging a seed into a crevice, then hacking the seed open with the chisel-like bill. We can find red-breasted nuthatches in mature conifers, where they extract seeds from cones. They visit feeding stations where they will quickly grab a sunflower seed and fly off to "hack" it open. Having powerful legs and feet they can climb down tree trunks head first.

BUNCHBERRY is found in the upper half of Minnesota except for the westernmost counties. Its preferred habitat is a cool, moist, coniferous forest where the plant often grows in colonies. The subtle taste of the berries is enjoyed by hikers in August and September. Thrushes, vireos, and grouse also eat the berries.

photo: David Brislance

Female red-breasted nuthatch on a tree fungus called artist's conk, and bunchberry with orange-red ripe fruit, near Lutsen.

photo: Jim Gilbert

Wildlife photographer David Brislance hand-feeding a black-capped chickadee friend at Lutsen.

photo: David Brislance

photo: David Brislance

AUGUST

The male **PURPLE FINCH** (above) is washed with a raspberry red (not purple). It's a summer resident in northern Minnesota and a widespread winter visitant throughout the state. It feeds mostly up in trees on seeds and berries, but also visits bird feeders.

FIREWEED (left) is one of the first plants to grow after a forest fire, thus its common name. But fireweed doesn't need a wildfire, it can grow as a pioneer plant on any disturbed site, including roadsides, railroad grades, and even urban ruins. It's fairly common in the northern part of the state and abundant in areas of the BWCAW recently devastated by fires. The rose-purple flowers open individually from the bottom of the spike up, taking several weeks to reach the top. There's an old saying: "When fireweed blooms to the top, summer is over."

photos: Jim Gilbert

A common understory tree, the **PIN CHERRY** (above) occurs throughout the forested regions of the state, especially northward. It has attractive, shiny red berries that ripen in July and August. They are an important wildlife food and also make a tart jelly.

A SOLDIER BEETLE (above) feeds on the pollen and nectar of a CANADA GOLDENROD. A tall, native wildflower that tends to grow in patches, Canada goldenrod is often seen in meadows and along roadsides throughout the state. The use of goldenrods as summer and fall flowers in perennial gardens is becoming quite popular. The flowers are bright yellow and full of nectar that attracts bees, flies, beetles, and butterflies. Their pollen, which is sticky and heavier than most windblown pollen, is carried by these insects from one flower to the next. Because very little goldenrod pollen gets into the air, these plants are not considered hay fever plants.

The CHOKECHERRY (right) is a native that grows as a tall shrub or small tree throughout Minnesota on lakeshores and borders of woods. The fruit is ripe from mid-July to late August and eventually turns purplish-red to blackish. A favorite of wildlife, the fruits are often harvested for jelly.

photos: Jim Gilbert

SERVICEBERRIES (left) make up a complex group of deciduous shrubs and small trees. About two dozen species are found in North America, and eight of them are native to Minnesota. Three common names are used for these woody plants—serviceberry, shadbush, and Juneberry.

The name serviceberry came into use during the nineteenth century because these plants bloom in mid-April in New England, when snow-covered roads became passable and long-delayed religious services were held once again. "Shadbush" comes from the fact that the plants usually bloom when the shad are running up the rivers of New England to their spawning grounds. And Juneberry is used because in many parts of the United States the fruit ripens in June.

The serviceberries are at their best in mid-spring, before or just as their leaves appear; at that time they produce masses of small white flowers with five narrow petals spreading to about an inch in diameter. In the fall these plants draw our attention once again as their leaves turn to brilliant yellows and reds.

But in midsummer, it's the fruit that interests us most. The fruit on all types of serviceberries is edible. The reddish-purple, and sometimes almost black, quarter-inch berries were an important source of food for various American Indian tribes. The fruit may be eaten fresh or used for puddings, pies, jelly, and wine. While out on walks in southern Minnesota in June, I like to pick handfuls of those sweet, juicy fruits, which typically grow in clusters of 6 to 12. Up along the North Shore we don't enjoy this treat until August. The berries are also an important wildlife food, sought out by cedar waxwings, American robins, and other birds, as well as chipmunks and red squirrels. Even black bears relish serviceberries.

These **GREAT EGRETS** and one **GREAT BLUE HERON** (left) gathered in a wetland just west of Lake Waconia on August 7, 2011. The great egret is a slim, all-white heron, 40 inches tall, with long black legs and a long yellow bill. This elegant wader is often seen standing like a statue along the edge of a lake or pond, looking for a fish to spear with its sharp bill. Other food consists of frogs, crayfish, and aquatic insects. They nest in colonies that may include a hundred individuals. One of the most magnificent of our herons, the great egret has fortunately recovered from near-extinction. In the late nineteenth century, colonies of this majestic bird were slaughtered indiscriminately by hunters in pursuit of the long white plumes that grow near the egret's tail during breeding season, which were considered a fashionable adornment to women's hats.

Wild RASPBERRIES are delicious, and to pick your own out in the brush is a special treat, though you might get a "rasp" from the stiff, bristly hairs on its branches.

These 3-foot shrubs often grow in dense thickets, as the plant spreads rapidly by long underground rhizomes (an underground stem producing roots and new fruiting stems). The shrub is common throughout Minnesota except in the southwest. It prefers full sunlight or partial shade, and thrives in a variety of dry to moist habitats, including young hardwood forests, meadows, swamps, lakeshores, and woodland edges. The fruits, which ripen in July and August, are important food for wildlife. Dozens of bird species, including ring-necked pheasant, gray catbird, northern cardinal, pine grosbeak, American robin, and brown thrasher, are prominent among the long list of creatures that enjoy the juicy berries. They're also popular with black bears, raccoons, chipmunks, and squirrels. The thickets of raspberry canes offer cover and nesting sites for birds, rabbits, and other animals.

Found throughout Minnesota in forest areas, the EASTERN CHIPMUNK (right) is a small squirrel that gathers and stores large amounts of seeds, nuts, and dried berries in an underground cavity connected to its living chambers. They eat from this cash during the winter, between short periods of hibernation. HAZELNUTS are an important chipmunk food; gray squirrels and other animals also eat them. Moose and deer eat the twigs and foliage of hazel, and grouse eat the buds and catkins.

Two species of hazel shrubs live in the state. Both are abundant as forest understory shrubs and produce nuts encased in leafy husks. The husk that surrounds beaked hazelnut has a long tube; American hazel has broad fringe at the end of the husk. The nuts of both species mature in late summer or autumn. They are edible. Just remove the husk, shell, and eat as is, or use in any recipe calling for nuts. The filbert is a cultivated form of hazelnut.

[photo: David Brislance]

Anja and Ailsa Gilbert picking wild red raspberries (right) at Lutsen.

photos: Jim Gilbert

The **THIMBLEBERRY** (below), a thornless 4-foot shrub with maple-like leaves, occurs here and there throughout northeastern Minnesota, but is common only in forests near the shore of Lake Superior. The conspicuous 2-inch white flowers are seen in June into July, and the fruits ripen to red in August. The berries are rather tart and dry but quite edible; they're soft, raspberry-like, and can easily fit over a finger like a thimble. Energetic pickers can gather enough of the berries to make delicious pies or jam.

The giant garden **SUNFLOWER** is related to the native annual sunflower that was first cultivated by Native Americans for its edible seeds. In nature the flowers are only a few inches in diameter, but cultivated varieties sometimes exceed 12 inches across. The plants easily grow 8 or 9 feet tall. A massive flower head, made up of hundreds of small brown disk flowers, is surrounded by yellow flowers called ray flowers. Although flowers normally serve to produce seeds, the ray flowers (banner flowers) of the sunflower are sterile; apparently their only function is to attract insects. So the disk flowers in the center of the head, each one small and inconspicuous in itself, attend to pollination and the production of seed.

photos: Jim Gilbert

John James Audubon called hummingbirds "glistening fragments of the rainbow," and most birders agree that they're the gems of the bird world. By August the RUBY-THROATED HUMMINGBIRDS (right) have begun their feeding frenzy. Now is the time to set up several feeders, widely spaced, as there are twice as many of these tiny birds. The newborns have joined the adults in our gardens and at feeding stations, and because their fall migration period begins in early August, we in the southern part of Minnesota begin to notice more hummers, always by mid-August. Some observers say that in mid to late August the hummingbirds are in the gardens more than they are at the feeders. Here the cardinal-flower and other tubular red flowers, blooming hostas and hollyhocks, and small insects are abundant sources of food.

photo: David Brislance

The HENDERSON HUMMINGBIRD HURRAH is held the third weekend in August every year to celebrate Minnesota's smallest bird. Some of the activities include mini-workshops on bird biology and conservation, gardening for hummingbirds, and hummingbird banding. Here hummingbird biologist Don Mitchell and volunteer Connie Marnie release a bird. Mitchell offered several sessions on banding at the 2011 festival, and several hundred people got the opportunity to sit on bleachers and watch him place minute rings on the tiny birds, all the while answering questions from the audience. Don has banded more than two thousand hummingbirds. He recaptured a female ruby-throat in his Red Wing yard 6 years after banding it; she was an adult when originally banded so she was at least 7 years old. The bird's average life span is 4 to 5 years, if it makes it through the first year. Four of our native plant species in Minnesota rely on hummingbirds for pollination—the cardinal-flower, spotted touch-me-not, columbine, and Indian paintbrush.

photo: Jim Gilbert

photo: David Brislance

photo: Jim Gilbert

ADULT BLACK BEARS (left) live solitary lives, except during June mating season. Females usually breed every two or three years. Mother bears with cubs can be very dangerous, and hikers must be wary of them. If a mother bear thinks that someone is threatening her cubs she could attack. Just be respectful of a bear's space and there won't be any problems. Average adult bears weigh 150 to 325 pounds, are about 5 feet long and stand 3 feet tall. They can run up to 30 mph for short distances, are powerful swimmers and good tree climbers.

The WHITE ADMIRAL BUTTERFLY (right) is also called the banded purple butterfly. This newly emerged, 3-inch specimen (August 22, 2011) is from the second brood, which is on the wing from August into September in northern Minnesota. They will nectar on forest flowers and also eat tree sap, rotting fruit, dung, and honeydew from aphids. Note the white bands across the middle of the black wings, the blue spots on the margins, and brick-red spots on the hind wings. Host plants for their caterpillars include birches, willows, and aspens, and also leaves from some other hardwood trees and shrubs.
[photo: David Brislance]

COMMON TANSY (left) is a wild plant in Europe and occurs as an escape from cultivation in North America. It grows in old fields and along roads throughout the state and is frequently seen along the North Shore. This 3-foot-tall perennial has finely divided feathery leaves topped by clusters of rayless, half-inch-wide, bright yellow button-like flower heads. The leaves have a strong medicinal odor. Not surprisingly, the plant has been used in many folk remedies, although usually with poor results because it contains a toxic oil.

Swimming days end, steam fog rises from lakes on cold mornings, and frost can strike at any time. Yes, September is a transition month, the month of summer's ending. The first few days of September are definitely summer, but the last days are truly autumn. The green prime is passing and we're coming up to the grand finale of the growing season, the color-splashed autumn foliage. Dozens of apple varieties become ripe, the last of the sweet corn is harvested, chrysanthemum and garden rose flowers are superb, black walnuts and Ohio buckeye nuts fall, and wild mushroom hunting is excellent. Northern flickers flock for migration. Rafts of American coots return to southern Minnesota lakes, while Hawk Ridge in Duluth becomes the best place to see fall hawk migrations. Moose in northern Minnesota shed velvet from their antlers.

During the first half of September, the commercial and garden grape harvest is underway. Fall-bearing raspberry canes produce much ripe fruit. Apple growers harvest Wealthy and SweeTango, plus Chestnut crabs. Fields of soybeans turn golden-yellow as the plants mature. Farmers could harvest their fourth crop of alfalfa and begin chopping corn for silage.

The loudest and most constant sound of the animal world at this time comes from various cicadas, grasshoppers, and crickets. Some species sing during the day and others at night. We see green darner dragonflies, monarch butterflies, and common nighthawks heading south. Wood ducks, wild turkeys, blue jays, black bears, and white-tailed deer are among animals eating recently fallen acorns. The wild rice harvest is well underway in the central and northern parts of the state, where common loons are also gathering on the

SEPTEMBER

larger lakes before migrating to the Gulf Coast or Atlantic seaboard.

Most ruby-throated hummingbirds leave northern Minnesota by September 12 and the southern part of the state by September 25. Be sure to keep those sugar water feeders up until you're certain the hummers have all left; that could be into October. Ruby-throats usually migrate by day but they can also migrate at night. Their wintering locations range from south Texas to Costa Rica.

The last half of September, Virginia creeper vines are draped through trees and on fences like red garlands. Along roadsides, sumac shrubs exhibit their mostly red foliage. Green ash and eastern cottonwood trees are glowing with golden-yellow foliage. Common milkweed pods have begun opening. Apple growers pick Macintosh, Red Baron, Honeycrisp, and Cortland apples. White-tailed deer have changed to their gray-brown winter coats. In south, central, and western Minnesota, potato, sugar beet, and soybean harvesting is underway. Fall colors are especially showy across the northern tier of the state. Bears in the northeast have started heading for hibernating spots.

photos: David Brislance

The orange and black **EASTERN COMMA BUTTERFLY** (above) has a 2-inch wingspan. It will hibernate through the winter months, rather than spending them as a chrysalis, caterpillar, or egg. Adults do not usually go to flowers, but take in nutrients and moisture from wet soils, tree sap, rotten fruit, and decaying organic matter. The liquids are sucked into the mouth through a slender straw-like tube called a proboscis. An individual eastern comma, like the one in the photo, will hibernate in a hollow tree or other locality, out of the wind, rain, and snow, from October into late March or April. Eggs are laid on elms and nettles in the spring, and there will be two broods in the summer, with the second brood becoming the hibernators. When the butterfly perches in closed-wing pose, as well camouflaged as a dead leaf, it's quite easy to see a small silver-white comma on the underside of the hind wing.

HOMER LAKE (left) on the edge of the Boundary Waters Canoe Area in Cook County, September 6, 2008. This serene scene reminds us of the fact that the first few days of September are usually summer-like. However, the maples and birches will soon be displaying their autumn splendor.

Western **POISON IVY** (below) grows as a knee-high shrub statewide. We came upon this dense patch, displaying beautiful fall colors, in early September near Park Rapids. The shiny leaves always have three leaflets, with the center leaflet featuring a longer stem. The plants grow in forest areas but also out in the open. Small, light-green flowers appear in June, and clusters of small, berry-like, pale-yellow fruits are ripe in September and hang on through the winter.

These common plants can be a nuisance to us humans because of the serious skin irritations they cause, but they're good groundcovers, are visually attractive, especially in fall color, and have considerable wildlife value. Included in the list of over fifty species of birds that eat the seeds are sharp-tailed grouse, ring-necked pheasants, wild turkeys, black-capped chickadees, northern flickers, yellow-bellied sapsuckers, white-throated sparrows, yellow-rumped and Cape May warblers, and several of the woodpeckers. Black bears and rabbits are among the mammals that eat poison ivy leaves, stems, and seeds.

It appears that only humans are susceptible to the toxic, oily compound that's carried in the plant's leaves, stems, roots, flowers, and fruits. In addition to direct contact between bare skin and plant, the irritant may travel on the fur of a dog or cat, camping equipment, garden tools, or clothing. The irritating chemical is not volatile, but tiny droplets may be carried in smoke on dust particles. Such particles are sometimes inhaled, causing serious problems. The pollen is blown by wind, and it's possible for an extremely susceptible person to contact the poison merely by being near the plant when its pollen is in the air.

Sensitivity to poisoning can vary from person to person, and can change with time. Very few individuals are immune, and those that appear to be sometimes lose their immunity unexpectedly. The poison is absorbed into the skin almost immediately, causing itching, burning, redness, and small blisters to appear within a few hours or days. Washing with soap and cold water (warm water speeds the absorption through the skin) will often prevent or alleviate the symptoms if done within three minutes of exposure, and might also remove residual poisons and prevent the rash from spreading. The fluid in the blisters themselves does not contain the poison and cannot spread the rash.

photo: Jim Gilbert

A **SOYBEAN** field (below) on the outskirts of St Peter. I'm in the field with my Gustavus Adolphus College Environmental Studies class, experiencing first-hand the maturing soybean plants in early September. The soybean is native to China and Japan. In Minnesota, the nation's third-largest producer, this annual is seeded in during May and harvested from mid-September through October. Each 2-inch pod contains 2 to 4 seeds and each plant produces many pods. Hundreds of products are made from soybeans, including meal to feed farm animals and many of the foods we eat, such as breakfast shakes, tofu, soy milk, and veggie-burgers. The United States is now the world's leading consumer of soybeans.

Home-grown **FALL SQUASH** (above) for sale at At The Farm, on the east side of Waconia. The fall squashes, also called winter squashes, are usually baked or boiled, after which the flesh is scraped out. These late-growing squashes may have smooth, rough, or warty skin. The fruits can be oddly shaped but all winter squashes develop a hard rind that's conducive to good storage. Winter squashes probably originated in regions of Mexico and South America.

photos: Jim Gilbert

photos: David Brislance

Caribou Lake (above) near Lutsen. Fall colors coming on fast, September 13, 2006.

Wilson's warbler (left above) North Shore, September 3, 2008.

A lesser yellowlegs (left below) near Duluth.

photos: Mirceax|dreamstime.com

My daily journal entries during the first few days of September each year are full of notations on bird migrants seen including flycatchers, red-breasted nuthatches, shorebirds, common nighthawks, and about 20 species of warblers. Among the wood warblers typically seen are Cape May, magnolia, Tennessee, black-throated green, Nashville, and Wilson's. Most Wilson's warblers nest in the woodlands of Canada. This species breeds sparingly in extreme northeastern Minnesota, but they are encountered in northern and southern parts of the state during migration. They are a 5-inch bird with olive-green above and yellow below, and a black cap. Females and young males lack the cap. Wilson's warblers winter from Mexico to Panama.

photo: Jim Gilbert

The first migrating **American coots** returned to Lake Waconia for the fall season on September 13 in both 2009 and 2010. In 2011 the first raft arrived on September 14. By late September, and through October into November, we'll see big numbers of these birds, sometimes in huge flocks of a thousand or more on some southern Minnesota lakes.

American coots are about a foot long; they're charcoal gray with blacker head and a thick white bill. Both sexes look alike. Coots are the most aquatic members of the rail family, moving on open water like ducks and feeding with them.

An American coot nods its head as it swims. I enjoy hearing their voices—a varied chorus of clucking and chattering notes. Coots are excellent swimmers and divers. These birds must patter over the water with their wings flapping to become airborne. They eat various aquatic plants and some insects, and will also come up on land to feed on seeds and grasses. When they do, you may be able to see their green legs and big feet with lobes along the toes—better suited to swimming than walking. They winter in southern states, Mexico, and Central America.

FALL FRUIT

photos: Jim Gilbert

Ohio buckeye (top) and European mountain ash specimens at the Linnaeus Arboretum at Gustavus Adolphus College in St. Peter.

The **OHIO BUCKEYE** (above left) is a native tree from Pennsylvania to Alabama and west to Kansas, and has also been widely planted throughout Minnesota. It's known for its attractive spring flowers, dark green leaves composed of five to seven leaflets, and shiny seeds called buckeyes. Both children and adults find the nuts irresistible when they fall from the trees in mid-September. But don't eat them: all parts of the Ohio buckeye tree are considered toxic. Just enjoy carrying the rich brown buckeyes around in your pocket as a sign of the autumn season. The foliage changes to a pumpkin-orange soon after the seeds fall.

The **EUROPEAN MOUNTAIN ASH** (below left) was introduced to North America during colonial times, and was probably brought to Minnesota in the 1850s or a bit later. Often recommended for wildlife plantings, it is most often used as a specimen tree in a residential yard, where cedar waxwings and American robins eat much of the fruit. In September the fruits are orange, turning more reddish in October. The compound leaves change to yellow and red in the fall.

Originally **APPLES** (opposite page) grew wild in the area of the Black and Caspian seas. Now more than a hundred varieties of apples are grown in Minnesota, each with its own special flavor, texture, and sweetness or tartness. Many new apple varieties have been developed at the University of Minnesota Horticultural Research Center, including the popular Haralson apple in 1922. A few of the apple varieties that are ripe in mid to late September include: Wealthy, Red Baron (1969), Sweet Sixteen (1978), Honeycrisp (1991), SnowSweet (2000), and McIntosh. Bracketed years represent when an apple variety was introduced by the University. The Wealthy apple, Minnesota's oldest variety (introduced in 1873) was developed by Peter Gideon who lived near Lake Minnetonka in the Excelsior area. McIntosh was discovered in 1796 as a chance seedling of unknown parentage in Ontario, Canada.

The apple season in Minnesota can run from late July into November. An apple contains about 85 percent water, vitamins A and C, plus minerals and fiber, which makes it a healthy snack or part of a meal. [photo: Jim Gilbert]

photos: Jim Gilbert

The **DAHLIA** is a showy late summer and early fall flower. Its blossoms range from 1 to 18 inches across, in colors from white to yellow to red and purple, with many variations and combinations in between. Plants can range from 2 to 8 feet tall and need to be staked. Dahlias are tender tuberous-rooted plants. The tubers must be dug after the first frost and stored until spring in a cool, dry place with a temperature near 40 degrees F. These dahlias are blooming at the University of Minnesota Landscape Arboretum.

A tagged **MONARCH BUTTERFLY** (right) nectaring on New England aster near Waconia. Monarchs continue their travels through the state during September and into October. At an average flight speed of 11 miles per hour, the first ones reach their wintering sites in the mountain forests west of Mexico City close to November 1. I have been tagging monarchs and studying their migration and feeding behavior since the early 1970s.

OBERG **M**OUNTAIN (opposite page) which peaks at about 1,000 feet, offers views of Lake Superior, the Sawtooth Mountain Range, scenic Oberg Lake, and the surrounding sugar maple-covered landscape. Around the 25th of September each year, photographers, landscape painters, and others who are mesmerized by nature's handiwork are drawn here to experience the fleeting pleasure of truly spectacular autumn colors. This photo was taken on September 27, 2010. Sugar maples are ablaze with red and burnt-orange, paper birches display golden-yellow, and moose maple foliage is red, orange, and yellow.

To reach the 2.25 mile Oberg Trail, take Highway 61 about 5 miles northeast from Tofte, go north (left) on Onion River Road for 2 miles to the parking area and trailhead.

Other areas with great fall color at this time include the Gunflint Trail, International Falls, the Iron Range, and the wooded countryside around Thief River Falls. [photo: David Brislance]

photo: David Brislance

photo: John Toren

It's migrating time for the SHARP-SHINNED HAWK (left) and many other birds of prey. In September, birders from the Upper Midwest and other parts of the globe come to watch these birds at HAWK RIDGE in Duluth (above). Thousands of birds pass over this ridge during their migration to wintering areas as close as southern Minnesota or as distant as South America, to avoid crossing the vast expanse of Lake Superior and also to take advantage of the updrafts that develop along the ridge. After passing Hawk Ridge they quickly disperse.

The biggest flights usually occur between September 8 and 23, especially when skies are clear and winds are from the northwest, although the migration continues intermittently through November. Fourteen species of raptors are regular migrants over the Ridge, sharp-shinned and broad-winged hawks prominent among them.

During the summer, heavily forested areas throughout the state see an influx of **YELLOW-BELLIED SAPSUCKERS.** These woodpeckers are mottled with black and white, have a red forehead and crown, and a faint yellow tinge on the belly. The male also has a red throat.

Sapsuckers drill rows of "sap wells" through tree bark into the wood, returning often to lap the sap with their extremely long tongues and also to eat the insects attracted to the sap. These holes are also used as sources of food by several other birds and by mammals and insects. Unfortunately, sapsucker holes also damage trees and provide points of entry for fungus and other tree diseases. Their fall migration peaks in late September.

PEARLY EVERLASTING (above) is a common 2-foot tall perennial wildflower of the North, often growing where there have been forest fires. It's sometimes picked and dried for fall and winter bouquets.

The MOUNTAIN MAPLE behind it is the state's only native maple that develops into a shrub. It grows in the understory of forests throughout most of northern Minnesota, where it's also known as moose maple and browse maple because moose devour large quantities of it in early summer.

(right) A Forest Service road off the Sawbill Trail, Cook County, September 25, 2008: sugar maples and paper birches on display.

photos: David Brislance

Fishing amid the barges on the Mississippi River, just upstream from Winona.

photo: John Toren

October is the month of clear skies. We can expect frost several times, and Indian summer days after those frosts, with above-normal temperatures and little or no wind. These warm, sunny, hazy days always follow autumn's first frost and occur when high pressure dominates. And then, maybe, a few snow flurries.

October is also the time the woods put on a display. The maples go red and the foliage on eastern cottonwoods and paper birches turn golden-yellow, while both red and white oaks turn a variety of dark reds and rich browns—just a few examples of nature's extravaganza. Leopard frogs head for lakes and ponds where they'll hibernate in the mud. Before sunset, red-winged blackbird flocks gather in wetlands for the night; their trilling songs offer a haunting echo of spring. Muskrats add plant materials such as cattail stems and leaves to their domes. The potato and sugar beet harvest continues. Orchardists pick apples and farmers combine soybeans and corn. Tulip bulbs can be planted throughout the month for bloom next spring.

During the first week in October more flocks of dark-eyed juncos and large rafts of American coots arrive. Waves of American robins migrate through, and common tree frogs hang out on zinnias and other garden blossoms, approaching our lighted windows at night to look for insects. Asian ladybugs gather in numbers. The drive between Park Rapids, Walker, and Bemidji is beautiful; sumacs, birches, woodbine, red oaks, red maples, and highbush cranberry

OCTOBER

shrubs display their autumn splendor.

We expect the overall fall color peak in the Twin Cities and the countryside around Spicer, Mankato, Northfield, and Rochester in the second week of October. At that time grackles are seen in big flocks. Banded woolly bear caterpillars scurry across roads. Fireside, Haralson, Keepsake, and Regent are among the late-season apples being harvested. Brussels sprouts, broccoli, cabbage, cauliflower, and leaf lettuce continue to grow in the cooler weather. By the third week in October, it's time to put garden rose canes underground, but we continue to enjoy the blooming chrysanthemums.

The end of October is a perfect time to walk through crunchy leaves in the woods and enjoy the special aroma. The peak of the leaf-raking season has been reached. Leaves can be shredded with a power mower and then left on a lawn or put in flowerbeds and vegetable gardens to enrich the soil and help hold moisture. A few chipmunks are still running about but most are safely in their underground burrows.

photo: John Toren

JAPANESE SILVER GRASS (above right) is an ornamental grass known for its silver-white plumes in the autumn landscape. It's also called Miscanthus grass. The plums are feathery, fan-shaped, former flower stalks that are now fruit-seed stalks. A perennial native to marshes, slopes, and other open habitats, mainly in eastern Asia, this 6-foot grass is now commonly seen in southern Minnesota gardens. Japanese silver grass is easily propagated by seed or division, and a single clump will increase in size slowly each year, so it ends up growing on its own and will naturalize in sunny environments.

QUAKING ASPENS (right) in golden-yellow, amid birch and maple on the hills above the North Shore. This native aspen grows to a height of 45 feet, is the most abundant tree in Minnesota, and is known for its attractive autumn foliage.

photo: Calamityjohn | Dreamstime.com

The **HERMIT THRUSH** (right) is a fine singer but a shy forest bird, with bold spots, a distinct eye-ring, and a reddish tail that it frequently flicks. Smaller than a robin, the hermit thrush feeds on insects during the warm months and can subsist on berries and buds during fall and winter. Hermit thrushes nest in northeastern and north-central Minnesota, and are common spring and fall migrants throughout the state. Fall migration reaches its peak in mid-October, but there are stragglers into December, especially in the southern part of the state.

photo: David Brislance

photo: Jim Gilbert

The **SUGAR MAPLE** (left) is a common forest tree through-out much of Minnesota. By nature it's a slow-growing, long-lived tree that can become 60 or more feet tall. It commonly shares the forest canopy with basswoods and oaks. The leaves are broad, smooth-edged, and have five pointed lobes; they are dark green in summer and brilliant red or yellow in the autumn.

photo: Jim Gilbert

COMMON MILKWEED (right) grows in open places throughout most of Minnesota, though it's uncommon in the northeast. The flat seeds are wind-borne on tufts of silky hairs. Common milkweed is known for its milky juice. The early summer fragrant flowers, rich in nectar, attract a variety of insect pollinators. Its elliptical leaves are an important food source for monarch butterfly caterpillars.

photo: Jim Gilbert

RING-BILLED GULLS (above) are our most common gull, though most migrate to southern states and Mexico, with October being a prime migrating month. These gulls have a complete black ring on the yellow bill, yellowish legs and feet, and white spots on the black wing tips. They have close to a 4-foot wingspan. They eat insects and fish, and also scavenge in landfills and at fast-food restaurants, giving them the name French-fry gull. They are equally at home on ocean beaches, lakes, and rivers.

A native shrub that can reach 10 feet in height, the RED-OSIER DOGWOOD (right) grows abundantly in wet soils throughout most of the state. The flexible stems are bright red in autumn, winter, and early spring, and the leaves turn to striking red tones in October.

photo: David Brislance

SOYBEANS (left) ready for harvest. Standing soybeans and corn need to be down to 13 to 14 percent moisture content so they can be combined and then stored without further drying. By the third week in October, statewide, farmers have most of the soybean crop combined, and have started the combining of corn. It was not until the early 1900s that the soybean became a well-known farm plant in the United States. Now the U.S. is the world's biggest producer and also its largest consumer of soybeans. [photo: Jim Gilbert]

This grove of RED MAPLE trees (above right) is at peak of fall color, as noted by my environmental studies students here at Gustavus Adolphus College. The red maple is quite common in hardwood and coniferous forests throughout most of central and northern Minnesota. It grows well on both sandy and wet soils where sugar maples are likely to fail. The leaf shape is similar to other maples, but the leaf margins have more teeth than those of the sugar maple.

Timberlake Orchard (right) is located 9 miles south of Fairmont near the Iowa border. Orchardist Eric Luetgers here demonstrates to students from Gustavus Adolphus College the correct way to harvest APPLES. He also gave them a quick lesson in apple biology, pointing out that apples are pollinated by insects—that's why he keeps honey bees—and that the only job an apple tree has is to produce seeds. Ten seeds are produced in each fully developed apple. Eric also explained how he and his family care for the 4,500 apple trees in his orchard and gave us some insights on the business of marketing and selling 30 varieties of Minnesota apples.

photos: Jim Gilbert

AMERICAN BITTERSWEET (left) is a native vine found throughout most of the state on woodland margins and in brushy thickets. Formerly common, it has now become scarce is regions where motorists stop to harvest the branches in the fall.

Bittersweet has neither tendrils nor aerial roots, but climbs by twining its entire stem around the trunk of a tree or fence post. The fruit is an orange capsule that opens to display a cluster of bright red-orange seeds, each with a fleshy covering. These seeds hang on through winter or until birds such as wild turkeys, robins, or bluebirds eat them.

American bittersweet has become a popular planting on garden fences and is often used in holiday decorations, but in order to produce the colorful fruits, both male and female forms must be planted.

photos: Jim Gilbert

The GINKGO TREE is known as a living fossil because its close relatives lived at the time of the dinosaurs, 150 million years ago. Although they later disappeared from the North American continent, Ginkgo trees persisted in China, where they were cultivated in temple gardens and managed to survive. In the eighteenth century, Western botanists spotted the trees and brought seeds back to Europe. The tree was reintroduced into the United States in about 1784.

The ginkgo is now often grown as a boulevard tree because it tolerates air pollution and is quite resistant to insect damage and the usual tree diseases. It grows to about 45 feet in southern Minnesota. The glossy green leaves, mostly bi-lobed, are fan-shaped with veins radiating out in the leaf blade. In autumn, the leaves turn a bright yellow.

OCTOBER

A good share of the corn is harvested the second half of October, when the kernels have dried. Corn is the number one field crop in the United States. Before World War II most corn in the U.S. was harvested by hand, and it still is in many other countries. The corn combine was not widely adopted until after the war. Corn is grown on every continent except Antarctica.

125

An **AMERICAN TREE SPARROW** (below) feeds from a Canada goldenrod seed cluster. A migrant that nests in northern Canada and Alaska and winters in the northern states south to Arkansas and north Texas, the American tree sparrow is a common winter visitant at southern Minnesota feeding stations, where it prefers millet and cracked corn spread on the ground.

At a banding station where I worked in Carver Park Reserve we had individual American tree sparrows return winter after winter. Their peak migration time throughout the state is during October. To identify this handsome sparrow note the single dark spot or "stickpin" on the breast, and the red-brown cap. The bill is dark above and yellow below. Males and females look alike.

A pair of **RED-BREASTED NUTHATCHES** (above) have arrived to eat sunflower seeds from Jean Brislance's hand. Jean is an avid birder who has observed a good share of the 314 species of birds regularly seen in Minnesota each year. The red-breasted nuthatch, a permanent resident in the northeastern and north-central regions of the state, is one of about 100 bird species that spend the winter here.

These 4½-inch birds have a blue-gray back, prominent black eye stripes, and rusty underparts. Some of them migrate to the southeastern and south-central regions of the state in the fall, where they sometimes appear at feeding stations during the winter. Seeds from conifers are their principal year-round food. Like the slightly larger white-breasted nuthatch, the red-breasted have powerful legs and feet which make it possible for them to climb both up and down tree trunks and even walk along the bottoms of horizontal branches.

photos: David Brislance

The LAPLAND LONGSPUR spends summers on the Arctic tundra of Canada and Alaska, and also in northern Europe and Asia. Some migrate into Minnesota in the fall, with the peak time being in October. Longspurs live in flocks on the ground. Winter flocks frequent plowed fields and pastures and are most often seen in the central and southern parts of the state. They are seed-eaters, and sparrow-like in size and color. "Longspur" refers to the elongated claw of the hind toe, and "Lapland" to part of their summer breeding grounds. This photograph is unusual in that the bird is standing on a carpet of moss and lichen which brings out the beautiful brown feather tones. More often, longspurs are almost invisible on the ground; often a whole flock will dart into the air as an observer approaches, only to disappear again when they land on nearly bare ground a few hundred feet away.

The peak migration time for the EASTERN BLUEBIRD is from late September into late October, when they're fairly common throughout most of the state. A few of them overwinter, mainly in the southeast, but also sporadically along the North Shore of Lake Superior. Fruit is their cold-season food. This bluebird was spotted feeding on a native mountain ash tree near Lutsen in late October.

Dark-Eyed Juncos are on the move in October. They migrate at night at very low altitudes in flocks of up to a hundred individuals. Other birds, including both American tree sparrows and fox sparrows, may accompany them. They're coming from their nesting grounds in the coniferous forests of Canada and extreme northern Minnesota, and they're heading for southern Minnesota and as far as the Gulf of Mexico, where they'll spend the winter in city parks and suburbs as well as in the countryside. In southern Minnesota, dark-eyed juncos are sometimes called snow-birds because soon after they arrive we can expect our first snowfall.

The dark-eyed junco is a medium-sized sparrow with dark gray plumage on its head, chest, and upper parts that contrasts with the white belly and the white stripes on the outer tail. Its eyes are dark and the bill a light pink. Females are a much lighter gray color and tend to look tan-brown above.

We see more of the dark-colored males than the lighter females in the winter in southern Minnesota; females are more common in the southern states. Males risk harsh winters in the northern states in order to get a head start on the journey back to their breeding grounds to stake out territories in the spring.

Juncos eat both insects and seeds. At our feeding station in Waconia, they relish the cracked corn and millet seeds we scatter on the ground. With a potential lifespan of over 10 years, it's likely that the junco under your feeder has spent previous winters as your backyard guest.

A dark-eyed junco sits amid golden-brown branchlets of a northern white cedar that fell as a natural pruning process.

White-tailed deer (right) are not as large as most people think. The back of an adult deer is seldom more than waist high to the average adult person. Typical weights in the autumn are 170 pounds for bucks and 145 for does.

Back in September, the bucks started to rub their antlers against young saplings, removing the velvet from the antlers and leaving scars on the tree trunks. They continue to rub long after the velvet is gone, no doubt to mark the edges of mating territories with a scent from a specialized gland on their foreheads.

By the middle of October, deer have begun their mating season in earnest, and the scrapes and rubs of rutting males can be spotted in the woods. A buck may scrape an area of ground less than a square yard with his hooves, marking the scrape with urine and scent from glands located on his hind legs. The scrape is a sign to other males that the territory is occupied, and to females that an interested buck is nearby.

In late October, as competition intensifies, disputes between males take the form of aggressive displays and foot-stomping, sometimes followed by threats and rushes, with head lowered toward a potential rival. On occasion, two bucks can actually crash antlers in a battle of physical supremacy, though such bouts rarely last more than 30 seconds. Mating season is over by early December, and most bucks shed their antlers in January or February—only to grow them again a few months later as spring approaches. [Photos: David Brislance]

A quiet November morning on the Boy River east of Leech Lake.

A month of great transition from the warm season to the cold, November often starts out like autumn, complete with lingering fall colors, but ends up wintery. It brings long, chilly nights with glistening stars and hooting owls. Some days are clear, with ocean-blue skies, while others are spread with clouds that produce some of the best sunrises and sunsets of the year.

During Indian Summer days, golf courses remain open, boaters take advantage of the still-open waters on lakes, and picnickers and walkers enjoy the sunshine. Birds continue their great migrations, and farmers labor to finish corn combining and other fieldwork. Cattail seeds drift on tiny parachutes in the increasingly low-angle sunlight, and the windblown silvery seed-heads of dandelions and common milkweed make a splendid sight. Homeowners mow their lawns for the last time, put in the storm windows, and cut and stack wood for the coming season. By the end of the month raccoons enter their sleeping dens and new ice appears.

During the first week in November, gardeners may still be cutting broccoli and pulling beets, leeks, and onions. The last painted turtles sun themselves on logs in ponds. Norway maples, weeping willows, and European larches continue displaying golden-yellow leaves; winged euonymus shrubs are rose-red and native red oaks show browns and reds.

By the second week in November, some gardeners cover rows of carrots with straw, so they can be dug when needed throughout

NOVEMBER

the winter. Weeping willow trees continue to display attractive golden-yellow foliage, which make them look like the 4th of July fireworks called golden-showers. The last of the huge flocks of red-winged blackbirds head south. Hooded mergansers, ring-necked ducks, northern pintails, green- and blue-winged teal, and hundreds of white pelicans, American coots, and tundra swans gather on the backwaters of the Mississippi River just south of Brownsville.

November 19 is the average date for lasting snow cover to appear in the greater Twin Cities area. And during the third week of November, fresh-cut Christmas trees start to appear on retail lots. Lake Pepin is a good place to see diving ducks such as lesser scaup, canvasbacks, redheads, and buffleheads. Pine siskins, purple finches, gray jays, red-breasted nuthatches, and black-capped chickadees commonly appear at birdfeeders in northern Minnesota.

As November ends we're reminded that immersion heaters, available commercially, keep birdbaths ice-free. Birds need water year-round, and other wildlife such as deer, red squirrels, and gray foxes will come for water, too.

In the southern part of Minnesota, jack rabbits have turned from brown to white, and in the northern part of the state the snowshoe hares have also changed from brown to white. It's time for many ponds and lakes to freeze over.

Many varieties of CRABAPPLE TREES (right) have small colorful apples that cling to the trees, adding interest to fall and winter landscapes. Flocks of cedar waxwings often alight to feast on the apples; so do lingering flocks of American robins. Ring-necked pheasants, ruffed grouse, blue jays, and at least a dozen other bird species are fond of crabapples, as are deer, red foxes, raccoons, and squirrels.

Combining CORN (above). Farmers continue working hard through November to get the corn crop in and complete other fieldwork. In a typical year, 98 percent of the Minnesota corn crop is harvested by the end of the month.

photo: Jim Gilbert

The COMMON WITCH-HAZEL (left) is a shrub that sometimes reaches a height of 15 feet. It's native to deciduous forests in the eastern United States, though it only grows naturally in Minnesota's extreme southeastern counties. However, in other parts of southern Minnesota it's sometimes used as a landscape plantings because of its attractive yellow leaf color and its late bloom, which continues into November. The 1-inch, yellow, ribbon-like flowers often linger on, even after the leaves fall.

photo: Jim Gilbert

Late autumn sunrise over Lake Waconia. During November, because it's the month of clouds, we have the opportunity to enjoy many of the most beautiful sunrises and sunsets of the year.

photo: David Brislance

An American goldfinch in its somber winter plumage, on a white cedar branch, where it searches for seeds that may be lift in the cones.

132

Franklin's gulls returning to Lake Waconia at sunset. Between 4:45 and 5 PM they glide in steadily to roost for the night. For about two months each autumn, thousands of Franklin's gulls spend each night on the surface of the lake in an enormous white raft near the middle. In early November, big flocks of both Franklin's and ring-billed gulls follow farmers doing fall plowing to pick up worms and other small animals in the soil. Other southern Minnesota lakes are also nightly gathering spots for flocks of Franklin's gulls, also called "the prairie doves." By mid-November they leave for the Gulf Coast, and some winter as far south as Chile.

A Franklin gull in summer plumage.

photos: David Brislance

For several years David and Mary Brislance have been observing and feeding **FLYING SQUIRRELS** (left) at their home in the Lutsen area. During summer, about an hour after sunset, several arrive at their feeding station to dine on peanut butter, raw peanuts, and sunflower seeds. In winter they first appear soon after sunset. A spotlight fixed on the feeder makes viewing easier and doesn't keep them away.

Flying squirrels are about the same length as red squirrels but weigh less than half as much. Being nocturnal animals, they have large eyes. They also have loose folds of skin between their front and hind legs. A flying squirrel will climb to a high branch and hurl itself into space, extending its four legs outward in a fixed position so that these flaps of skin are stretched like wings. Thus, flying squirrels don't actually fly, but glide, always losing altitude, guiding themselves with their flat, bushy tail. Most glides are 25 to 50 feet and end at the trunk of another tree, though glides of over 150 feet have been observed.

Surprisingly, flying squirrels are likely to be the most abundant of the squirrels in forested parts of Minnesota and Wisconsin. They are quite social. In winter as many 30 of these squirrels have been found in one tree cavity.

The only true lark native to North America, the **HORNED LARK** (right) is a summer resident throughout most of the state except the forested portions of the north-central and northeast. It's a common fall migrant throughout the state including the North Shore. The horned lark has a huge range extending from the Arctic to South America, Eurasia, and North Africa. They live on the ground in plains and prairies, open fields, golf courses, airports, beaches, and tundra. Larger than a sparrow, this bird's yellow chin, black sideburns, and small black horns are distinctive. It also has a black crescent on the lower neck area. Horned larks eat both seeds and insects. They are one of the earliest spring migrants, with flocks moving into southern Minnesota in February.

photo: David Brislance

photo: David Brislance

A wave breaking at Grand Marais Light station. Big waves are produced by the infamous November storms on Lake Superior.

photo: Jim Gilbert

The **PINE MARTEN** (above) is a forest dweller whose range extends into Minnesota's northeastern corner. An omnivore, it eats pine seeds and berries but prefers small mammals such as squirrels and mice. Pine martens are roughly 2 feet long, including the tail. They are adept at climbing trees and live a mostly solitary life. The fur on their head, usually gray, is lighter in color than the brown body.

The **POPLAR RIVER** (right) near Lutsen, is one of about 200 rivers that flow into Lake Superior, the largest lake on earth by area. Evergreens such as pines, spruces, and firs add interest to the late autumn landscape.

In 2010, Lake Minnewashta (below) near Excelsior in Carver County, froze up on November 27. However, because the lake opened up again later, the official FREEZE-UP DATE that year wasn't until December 2. Freeze-up is the first day when at least 90 percent of a lake is frozen over and *stays* frozen over. Note the flock of Canada geese on the new ice. They will soon take off to find open water.

During the fall season, as the angle of the sun drops, lake water cools. As it cools it shrinks, becoming more dense. Once the temperature drops below 39 degrees F., however, the water begins to swell, and this cooler water, having become less dense as it swells, naturally rises to the surface. Ice forms at 32 degrees. On the first calm, freezing day or night after a particular pond or lake reaches 39 degrees in all parts, an ice cover will form. The temperature of the water in contact with the ice sheet is 32 degrees, but a few feet below the ice the temperature remains above freezing, reaching 39 degrees on the bottom.

photo: Jim Gilbert

NOVEMBER

photo: David Brislance

In the fall, flocks of **SNOW BUNTINGS** (left) roam over the open countryside in the Lutsen/Tofte area, often in the company of Lapland longspurs and horned larks. All three of these species blend into the ground so well that observers may not see a nearby flock until it takes flight. About the last week of October the first flocks return to Grygla, Grand Marais, and other parts of the state's northern tier, and soon flocks are also seen in southern Minnesota, where they prefer open areas such as farm fields, especially ones with freshly spread manure. They spend their summers on the Arctic tundra. These 6- to 7-inch insect-and-seed-eating birds are also found in Eurasia. No other songbird shows so much white. In autumn and winter some individuals may look quite brown, but when they fly their flashing white wing patches easily identify them. In summer the male snow bunting has a black back, contrasting with its white head and underparts.

A **SHORT-TAILED WEASEL** (left) in its white winter coat. Snowshoe hares, which live in the northern part of the state, and weasels that are found throughout the state, have turned white by the third week of November. They started changing from brown to white in October and now are looking for snow cover. Weasels in white are called ermines. [photo: David Brislance]

A typical November scene (right) from the Lutsen/Tofte area. The white bark of the **PAPER BIRCH** and clusters of orange fruit from a native **MOUNTAIN ASH** enhance this view.

photo: Jim Gilbert

A November snowstorm featuring heavy wet snow, with enough to shovel and plow. The normal total snowfall for the month of November is 5.1 inches.

photo: Jim Gilbert

photo: David Brislance

Being a "snowbird" and hardy, the DARK-EYED JUNCO (left) is at home in snowy landscapes. During winter, junco flocks gather in fields, open woods, and brushy clearings where they search for seeds. Individuals roost close together for safely and warmth. In southern Minnesota, juncos are among the most common winter birds, often visiting feeding stations.

A mature BALD EAGLE (right) has a 7-foot wingspan. Here we see one soaring on a November day in the Grand Marais area. From the North Shore south to Green Lake (near Spicer) and Lake Minnetonka, along the Minnesota River and the edges of the great Mississippi from the Twin Cities to Winona and beyond, bald eagles are often seen patrolling shorelines in search of a meal—fish, wounded waterfowl, or carrion. These flights are a common sight, especially at freeze-up time, throughout much of the state. [photo: David Brislance]

Skiing fresh December snow on the well-groomed trails at Theodore Wirth Park in Minneapolis.

December is considered the time of gentle snows, but the theme of the month is "growing cold." If we do have a storm, after it's over a hard cold sets in for several days. The intensity of the sunlight is now just a quarter of the maximum level we had back in June. A fresh snow-cover reflects close to 90 percent of the sun's radiation. No wonder we experience cold days! Daylight is at a minimum for the year, so many of us find ourselves heading off for work in the dark and returning home—also in the dark. The coldest part of the month is usually the last week.

Lakes continue to freeze over. Ice on lakes echoes with resounding moans and creaks as air temperatures drop. At this time untold millions of animals—including wood frogs, American toads, painted turtles, black bears, woodchucks, red admiral butterflies, wood ticks, and various mosquitoes—are hibernating across the region. Deer begin dropping their antlers. Ring-necked pheasants feed on corn stubble and pick up gravel along roadsides. The gravel goes into the gizzard which helps grind up food in the first stage of digestion. Screech owls often roost in wood duck houses. Gray squirrels and other animals also use these nesting boxes for winter shelter. Birdfeeder birds such as northern cardinals, nuthatches, and downy woodpeckers are numerous and active. Animal tracking in fresh snow is a fun activity.

The red fruit on sumacs, highbush cranberry shrubs, and many varieties of crabapple trees is very colorful. Northern white

DECEMBER

cedars and various spruces and pines each have their own shade of green. December is full of natural marvels, from an intricate snowflake, to a chickadee taking seeds from a human hand, to the sights of Orion and the Big Dipper on a cold, clear night.

Take time to celebrate the beauty and wonder.

Now that the mating season is over, **WHITE-TAILED DEER** continue their quest to survive. Deer have keen senses, including excellent eyesight and hearing, but like many mammals, they actually rely heavily on the sense of smell to understand their world. They are constantly sniffing the air.

Deer have strict territories, and most live within an area of 50 to 300 acres, depending on the food supply and amount of cover. Deer survive because they know their territories very well. If one is chased by a predator it stays within its territory, bounding on trails through familiar tree stands and brush. A deer can sprint close to 40 miles per hour.

Deer are constant browsers, and each winter day they eat five pounds of food for every 100 pounds of weight. They browse thin twigs for buds and new bark. Among their favorites are northern white cedar, sugar maple, basswood, sumac, and red-osier dogwood.

photo: David Brislance

photo: Jim Gilbert

New ice on Lake Waconia.

Soon after freeze-up, ice sheets on lakes are heard cracking, thundering, and rumbling. These loud, long roars and rolls don't necessarily mean that the ice is unsafe to walk on, but the eerie sounds remind us to respect the ice. Once liquid water turns to ice, it expands and contracts with the changing temperatures, causing the ominous booms.

It takes at least 4 inches of new solid ice in contact with stationary water for safe skating and ice fishing. A snowmobile requires 6 inches of ice, 8-12 inches are needed for a car or small truck, and 12-15 inches for a medium-sized pickup.

You don't want to fall through ice; cold water saps body heat 25 times faster than air of the same temperature. In 32° water, a person will last about 15 minutes before losing consciousness.

A camouflaged **SHORT-TAILED WEASEL** (below). These small, 4- to 5-ounce mammals usually hunt at night but in winter they can also be active during the day. They're generally solitary. They can kill animals several times their own weight, such as red squirrels and rabbits, and they also eat mice and insects. When wearing its white winter coat, this weasel is called an ermine. The coat is an adaptation for better hunting and to elude enemies in the snow. The short-tailed weasel is primarily a forest dweller, occurring throughout the state, but it's uncommon in the southwestern counties.

photos: David Brislance

The **ROUGH-LEGGED HAWK** (above) is an uncommon snowy-season visitor, mainly in the eastern half of the state. In the Sax-Zim Bog area of St. Louis County up to 40 such birds have been seen in an early winter. These relatively long-winged hawks, with a wingspan of 4.5 feet, weigh only 2.2 pounds. They spend summers in the Arctic where they hover easily above the tundra as they hunt small rodents.

photos: David Brislance

In December of 2011, David Brislance was in the Grand Marais area several times once again to see the waxwings. As in previous years, he was in awe while observing flocks of **Bohemian waxwings** and was able to photograph many individuals as they fed on the bright red-orange fruit of the native mountain ash.

These gregarious birds can be distinguished from the more common cedar waxwing by their larger size and also by the white and yellow markings on their wings. They move about in tight formations, calling to one another in faint, high-pitched shrieks before descending together on a tree or shrub to strip it of its fruit. The Bohemian waxwing can be found in the coniferous forests of Alaska, western Canada, and parts of Washington to Montana. They wander farther south and east irregularly during the winter.

photo: David Brislance

photo: David Brislance

The **NORTH SHORE** at Grand Marais. Through December, and most often all winter, Lake Superior stays open, but as winter progresses elegant patterns can form in the ice near shore and the beautiful blue tinges of the water's surface remind us again and again that "water is life."

photo: John Toren

Found throughout Minnesota, the **RED FOX** is omnivorous. It readily comsumes apples, berries, insects, fish, mice, and rabbits, and may also visit wildlife feeding stations to eat sunflower seeds, suet, dog food, and raw chicken scraps. Red foxes are quite shy and do not pose a threat to children or pets. Mated pairs will actually defend their territory from other foxes; however, they are often killed by coyotes or wolves. Red foxes weigh from 7 to 15 pounds.

R ED SQUIRRELS are active all winter. They prefer evergreen forests, which explains why they're far less abundant in southern Minnesota than in the north.

T his albino BLACK-CAPPED CHICKADEE (right) is a rare sight, indeed. It was photographed in the Sawbill Lake area, on the edge of the BWCA. With a heartbeat of 700 pumps a minute, black-capped chickadees need to eat the equivalent of their own weight each winter day. They are mainly seed-eaters. It would take 40 of these energetic wisps of life to weigh 1 pound.

photos: David Brislance

In December **SNOW** is still marvelous and elegant; it hasn't become commonplace and worn out its welcome. A fresh snowfall adds a new dimension to our neighborhoods as it covers our litter, heals the scars, and gives us soft beauty filled with wonder.

Snow on evergreen boughs is one of nature's most splendid sights.

photos: Jim Gilbert

149

photos: David Brislance

The **BOREAL CHICKADEE** (above) is a bird of the spruce-fir forest, ranging across Canada and into Alaska, and also found in northern New England. It's a year-round resident of northeast and north-central Minnesota. This one was spotted in the Sax-Zim Bog near Cotton in St. Louis County. Note the brown cap and rusty flanks. In size and behavior it's similar to the black-capped chickadee, though the boreal chickadee is more retiring and quiet than its curious and vocal cousin.

The **EVENING GROSBEAK** (left) is an 8-inch bird usually seen year-round only in the north-central and northeast part of the state. A member of the finch family, it's big, conical bill allows it to eat large seeds. Its diet includes tree seeds, like those from maples, ashes, and pines, along with insects in summer. At feeding stations evening grosbeaks prefer black oil sunflower seeds, peanuts, and safflower seeds spread out on large tray feeders. During some winters a few evening grosbeaks wander into far southern Minnesota.

About the size of a big crow, the 19-inch-long **PILEATED WOODPECKER** is a stunning black bird with a prominent red crest and white markings on the head and neck. An insect-eater that lives in the forested parts of Minnesota, they're secretive but widespread, sometimes appearing with a dramatic splash out of the deep woods. They're attracted to suet feeders, whether attached to a post or tree or suspended like the one pictured here.

photos: Jim Gilbert

The Gilbert yard and home near Lake Waconia.

Daylight is at its lowest ebb—8 hours and 47 minutes, if we don't count seconds—for the nine days between December 18 and 26. This is due to the earth's elliptical orbit. At this point in its revolution around the sun the earth has slowed and things aren't changing much. By December 27, the Twin Cities area will have regained a full minute of sunlight, and by January 1, we'll have four additional minutes to enjoy since those shortest daylight days.

Sunrise on Christmas morning at Lake Waconia (right). Forty years of statistics suggest that there is a 92 percent chance of a white Christmas with one inch or more of snow in International Falls, a 74 percent chance in St. Cloud, and a 72 percent chance in the Twin Cities.

Index

David Brislance is a wildlife photographer who lives with his wife, Mary, on a ridge above Lake Superior near Lutsen, Minnesota. His photographic interests center on observing and chronicling the wood warbler migrations, the ruffed grouse, the gray wolf, and the gray and red foxes. His bird and other animal images span all twelve months of the year in the Minnesota Arrowhead.

David grew up in Wanamingo, Minnesota, along the Zumbro River valley of southeastern Minnesota. He graduated from Luther College in Decorah, Iowa, attended the John Herron Art Institute in Indianapolis, Indiana, and taught art for thirty years in Isle, MN. He has been photographing wildlife on the North Shore for the last decade, and his works have appeared in a wide variety of regional publications.

photo: Jim Gilbert

photo: John Gilbert

Jim Gilbert is a consulting naturalist for WCCO Radio, coauthor of the Minnesota Weatherguide Environment Calendars since 1977, and the author of four books on nature in Minnesota. He writes a nature column which appears in several newspapers, and teaches part-time in the Environmental Studies Program at Gustavus Adolphus College in St. Peter, Minnesota, where he graduated in 1962.

Jim earned a master of natural science degree at the University of Oklahoma and later studied at several other institutions. For 30 years he served the Hopkins Public Schools as a science teacher and naturalist, retiring in 1998. Jim and his wife Sandy have three grown sons and are grandparents. Together they have hosted more than 20 ecotours to Costa Rica, Peru, Kenya, and other places. The Gilbert's live near the shore of Lake Waconia, 30 miles west of Minneapolis.